W9-AOK-454

ideals

Meatless Meals
COOKBOOK

by Donna M. Paananen

People have been eating meals without meat for thousands of years. For instance, Pythagoras, St. Francis of Assisi, Leonardo da Vinci, Benjamin Franklin, Percy Bysshe Shelley, George Bernard Shaw, and Mahatma Gandhi gave up meat. Today, more and more people in the United States are, for health reasons, either giving up meat entirely, or, at least, cutting their intake. Although some do occasionally eat fish, with an increased national interest in health, meatless meals are becoming more popular.

There is often a great deal of misunderstanding about eating a meatless diet. Some people believe you do not get enough protein, iron, and other nutrients without consuming meat each day. Others think that by giving up meat, only vegetables and fruits can be consumed. Still others believe that a vegetarian regime is time-consuming, or that the foods are uninteresting and unappetizing.

This book was written to dispel those beliefs. Cooking without meat can be delicious and exciting, less expensive, and healthier than the typical American high-cholesterol diet. We have included recipes using milk, cheese, butter, eggs, whole grains, and additional unrefined foods as an integral part of the diet. So, for a change of pace, try a meal without meat—you'll find it delicious!

the author

An *ideals* Publication

First Printing

ISBN 0-89542-619-6 295

Contents

OTHER COOKBOOKS AVAILABLE

All Holidays Cookbook
American Cookbook
Barbecue Cookbook
Christmas Cookbook
Christmas Gifts from the Kitchen
Cookie Cookbook
Country Bread Cookbook
Country Kitchen
Family Cookbook
Family Favorites from Ideals
Farmhouse Cookbook
Festive Party Cookbook
Fish and Seafood Cookbook
From Mama's Honey Jar
From Mama's Kitchen
Garden Cookbook
Gourmet on the Go
The Gourmet Touch
Guide to Microwave Cooking
Have a Gourmet Christmas
Junior Chef Cookbook
Menus from Around the World
Naturally Nutritious
Nice and Easy Desserts
Simply Delicious
Soups for All Seasons
Tempting Treasures
Whole Grain Cookbook

photo stylists
Pamela Wilke
Rose Ann Pfeifer

artwork by
Jim McGath

designed by
Michele Arrieh

Editorial Director, James Kuse
Managing Editor, Ralph Luedtke
Production Editor/Manager, Richard Lawson
Photographic Editor, Gerald Koser

DEDICATION

To my father, Oliver W. Jones, Sr., 1909-1977, who died as he lived, helping others.

Cover photograph:
Garden Harvest Casserole, p. 28

Photograph opposite:
Caponata, p. 9

Appetizers and Savory Snacks

MOM'S HOT OLIVE CHEESE PUFFS

Yield: 2 dozen

- 1 c. grated sharp Cheddar cheese
- 3 T. butter, softened
- ½ c. whole wheat pastry flour
- ¼ t. paprika
- ¼ t. salt
- 24 pimiento stuffed olives, well drained

Blend the cheese and butter together thoroughly. Sift flour with seasonings and add to cheese mixture. Combine thoroughly with pastry blender or fork. Drop dough onto waxed paper by teaspoonfuls. Wrap dough around each olive, covering completely. At this point you can freeze the wrapped olives (on a pan and when frozen, place in plastic bags), or bake immediately in a 400° oven on an ungreased baking sheet for 10 to 15 minutes or until lightly browned. Serve hot.

HERB SPREAD OR DIP

Yield: 2 cups

- 1¼ c. cottage cheese
- 1 6-oz. pkg. cream cheese (at room temperature), cut into chunks
- 2 T. chopped green onions
- 2 T. chopped parsley
- 2 T. chopped chives
- ⅛ t. thyme
- ¼ t. basil
- ¼ t. oregano
- ¼ c. plain yogurt (optional)
  Salt

Place cottage cheese and cream cheese into a blender. If mixture is too thick to blend, add yogurt. Add the rest of the ingredients and blend until mixture is smooth. Taste and add salt. Refrigerate several hours before serving. Goes well with Grandma's Onion and Poppy Seed Soda Crackers.

MARINATED MUSHROOMS AND CHICK-PEAS

Yield: 1⅔ cups

- 1 c. cooked chick-peas (garbanzo beans), drained
- ⅔ c. thinly sliced fresh mushrooms
- ¼ c. olive oil, or vegetable oil
- 2 T. cider vinegar
- 2 t. minced onion
- 1 t. basil
- 1 small garlic clove, minced
  Salt
  Freshly ground black pepper
  Parsley, minced (for garnish)

Place chick-peas and mushrooms into a small bowl. In a separate container, mix the rest of the ingredients, adding salt and pepper to taste. Pour marinade over chick-peas and mushrooms, tossing gently. Chill until serving time, tossing from time to time to marinate evenly. Serve garnished with a dusting of parsley.

CAROLYN'S GUACAMOLE

Yield: approximately 2/3 cup

- 1 ripe avocado, mashed
- 2 t. lime juice
  Onion salt
  Garlic salt
- 1 T. mayonnaise or sour cream

Mix all the ingredients together thoroughly; taste and correct seasonings. Add more mayonnaise if mixture doesn't "bind" well. Use as a dip with corn chips or as a sandwich spread.

SUNCHOKE STUFFED MUSHROOMS

Yield: 20 appetizers

20 large mushrooms, washed and patted dry
1 T. butter or margarine
¼ c. minced onion
1 large sunchoke (Jerusalem artichoke), scrubbed and grated
½ t. lemon juice
⅛ t. basil
⅛ t. oregano
Freshly ground black pepper
Salt
1 2-oz. pkg. feta cheese, mashed

Remove stems from caps of mushrooms. Chop stems and sauté them in butter with the onion and grated choke; add lemon juice. When onion begins to soften, add herbs; add salt and pepper to taste. Remove from heat. Meanwhile, rub butter onto each mushroom cap and place on lightly greased baking sheet. Preheat oven to 350°. Stuff each mushroom cap with choke mixture, top with mashed cheese, and bake 10 to 15 minutes or until mushrooms are cooked and cheese is melted. Serve immediately while hot.

ANTIPASTO

Choose from among the following to make an excellent, meatless antipasto:

Green or red pepper strips or circles
Olives
Mozzarella cheese cubes
Marinated garbanzo beans and mushrooms
Stuffed or plain celery ribs
Carrot sticks
Radish flowers
Caponata
Zucchini or patty pan squash circles (unpeeled)
Cucumber slices or sticks
Cauliflowerets
Cherry tomatoes
Pickled hot peppers
Hard-boiled egg slices or deviled eggs

Arrange choices attractively on a tray or on individual dishes and serve before meal with bread, if desired.

SAMOSA (INDIAN "PASTY")

Yield: 2 dozen

2 c. whole wheat pastry flour, sifted
2 T. butter, melted
1 T. ground coriander
¾ t. salt
½ c. warm water
1 lb. (about 3 medium) potatoes
1½ c. fresh or frozen green peas
1 T. vegetable oil
1 c. minced onion
1 yellow chili, seeded and chopped (or 1 or 2 green chilies)
1 t. chopped fresh ginger
1 t. cumin seed
2 T. chopped coriander leaves
1 t. curry powder
1 T. lemon juice or dry mango powder
2 T. whole wheat pastry flour
¼ c. water
Vegetable oil for deep frying

Mix flour thoroughly with butter, coriander, and salt. Add warm water slowly until a stiff but smooth ball of dough forms. Turn out onto lightly floured board and knead for about 5 minutes. Cover with a damp cloth and let rest for about 30 minutes. Meanwhile, scrub and quarter potatoes. Place in steamer basket and steam 20 to 25 minutes. Add green peas and steam 5 minutes or until potatoes are tender. Cool. When potatoes are cool enough, cut into small cubes. Sauté onion in a large skillet in the vegetable oil for about 2 minutes. Add the chili, all the seasonings, the potatoes, and the peas and cook about 5 minutes, stirring regularly. Let cool. Divide dough into twelve equal parts; shape into twelve balls. Roll into circles as thin as possible on lightly floured board with floured rolling pin. Cut circles in half. Divide filling among semi-circles, placing filling in the center. Brush edges of the semi-circles with the 2 tablespoons pastry flour mixed with ¼ cup water and seal carefully. Samosas should be shaped like quarter circles and have no loose edges. Heat vegetable oil to 360° for deep frying; fry samosas until golden. Drain on paper towels and serve immediately. Yogurt with fresh mint chopped into it is a good accompaniment.

LYNN'S CURRY-CHEESE CRACKERS

Yield: 30 crackers

1 c. whole wheat pastry flour
¼ t. salt
¼ t. dry mustard
¾ t. curry powder
　Dash of cayenne pepper
⅓ c. butter or margarine
½ c. grated sharp Cheddar cheese
1 egg, beaten
1 T. cold milk

Preheat oven to 400°. Combine first five ingredients. Cut in butter with a pastry blender until mixture resembles fine crumbs. Stir in cheese, egg, and milk. When mixture holds together, turn out onto floured board and roll to 1/16-inch thickness. Cut with floured 2-inch round cookie cutter; place on lightly greased baking sheets, and bake 6 to 8 minutes or until golden. Remove immediately to wire racks to cool. Store in airtight containers.

GRANDMA'S ONION AND POPPY SEED SODA CRACKERS

Yield: Approximately 7 dozen small crackers

3 c. whole wheat pastry flour
½ c. butter or margarine, chilled
½ c. minced onion
½ c. poppy seed
1 t. baking soda
¼ c. water
1 t. salt
2 t. cream of tartar
¼ c. cold milk (approximately)

Cut butter into flour with a pastry blender until mixture resembles crumbs. Add onion and poppy seed and mix well. Dissolve baking soda in water. Add soda mixture and remaining ingredients in order listed, stirring to form a dough. Turn out onto lightly floured surface. Preheat oven to 400°. Knead well for about 10 minutes. Roll out to ⅛-inch thick on a lightly floured surface with lightly floured rolling pin; cut with cookie cutters to desired shapes (or into squares or rectangles). Place on well-greased baking sheets, prick with fork if desired, and bake 6 to 8 minutes or until lightly browned. Remove from tins and let cool on wire racks. Store in tightly covered tins.

STUFFED CELERY

Yield: 12 to 15 celery ribs

12 to 15 celery ribs, washed
　Paprika (optional)

Trim end pieces of celery ribs, mince, and set aside. Add minced celery end pieces to stuffing. Smooth cheese stuffing into celery ribs; garnish with paprika, if desired. Cover and chill or serve immediately.

CHEDDAR CHEESE STUFFING

4 oz. Cheddar cheese, grated
4 oz. softened cream cheese
1 t. prepared mustard
　Dash of hot bottled pepper sauce

Combine all ingredients, mixing well.

ROQUEFORT STUFFING

1 4-oz. pkg. Roquefort or blue cheese
4 oz. softened cream cheese
1 t. Worcestershire sauce

Combine all ingredients, mixing well.

CHILI BEAN DIP

Yield: 2 cups

2 c. cooked kidney beans, drained, save juice
4 t. tomato juice
1 T. cider vinegar
1 t. Worcestershire sauce
2 or 3 garlic cloves
2 t. chili powder (to taste)
　Dash of cayenne pepper or liquid red pepper sauce
⅓ c. cubed Cheddar cheese
　Salt
　Freshly ground black pepper
　Chives (for garnish)

Place first seven ingredients into blender; cover and blend on high until smooth. Add bean cooking juice if mixture is too thick. Add cheese; blend until smooth. Taste and add seasonings. Pour into the top of a double boiler or a very heavy saucepan and heat until hot (or bake in a 350° oven for 15 to 20 minutes or until thoroughly heated through). Sprinkle chives on top. Serve with corn chips, vegetables, pita bread, etc.

Photograph opposite:
Chili Bean Dip

SESAME AND/OR CELERY CRACKERS

Yield: Approximately 6 dozen

¾ c. sesame seed (*or* twice as many if you're making sesame crackers only)
½ t. (or more) celery seed
3½ c. pastry flour, sifted
1 c. (2 sticks) margarine or butter
1½ t. salt
½ c. ice water

Toast sesame seed in a heavy frying pan over low heat, stirring regularly, until they are lightly browned. Let cool. Meanwhile, cut margarine into flour with a pastry blender or fork until mixture resembles crumbs. Add salt. Divide mixture in half if you're making both kinds of crackers. To half of the mixture add the cooled sesame seeds; to the other half add the celery seeds. Slowly stir in ¼ cup ice water to each half until dough is thoroughly moistened and will form a ball. Cover and chill for about 30 minutes. Preheat oven to 400°. Lightly dust two 11 x 7-inch baking sheets with flour. With a well-floured rolling pin, roll out dough directly onto baking sheets. (To get dough into corners evenly, use a floured drinking glass.) Patch if necessary and make certain dough is even from one end of baking sheet to the other. Cut dough into triangles, rectangles, or 2-inch squares. Prick dough with a fork. Bake 10 to 12 minutes or until crackers are lightly browned. Remove from baking sheets immediately, and allow to cool on wire racks. Store in tightly covered tins.

WHOLE WHEAT WALNUT BREAD WITH WALNUT CHEESE SPREAD

Yield: 2 loaves bread and approximately 1 lb. cheese spread

WHOLE WHEAT WALNUT BREAD

1 pkg. active dry yeast
¼ c. lukewarm water
2 c. cooled scalded milk
2 T. butter, melted
2 T. honey
2 t. salt
6 c. whole wheat flour
Butter
1 c. whole walnuts

Sprinkle yeast on water in a large mixing bowl and stir until yeast is dissolved. Add milk, butter, honey, salt, and 1 cup flour. Stir thoroughly until well blended. Stir in 3 more cups of flour, one at a time, mixing thoroughly after each addition. Add the fifth cup of flour, beating until mixture is stiff. Sprinkle a board with the last cup of flour and knead dough with floured hands until dough is smooth (about 10 minutes). Don't underknead. Place dough in a well-buttered bowl, turn once, cover, and let rise in a warm place (85°) until two fingers inserted in dough leave an indentation. Punch down, work in the walnuts. Shape into two round loaves and let rise until doubled in bulk on a well-greased baking sheet (for about 1 hour). Bake in a 375° oven for about 45 minutes or until done. Let cool on wire racks.

WALNUT CHEESE SPREAD

(make at least 1 day in advance)

1 4-oz. pkg. Brie, softened
1 4-oz. pkg. Camembert, softened
1 4-oz. pkg. Liederkranz, at room temperature
4 oz. cream cheese, softened
2 to 3 T. kirsch or cherry liqueur
½ c. whole walnuts, toasted in a frying pan

Beat the cheeses together until smooth; add kirsch and continue beating until well blended. Stir in walnuts. Let ripen 24 hours before serving with Walnut Bread.

CAPONATA
(EGGPLANT APPETIZER)

Yield: 8 ample servings

½ c. olive oil, *or* ¼ c. olive and
    ¼ c. vegetable oil
6 c. (1 large) eggplant, washed and cubed
1 c. diced celery
2 c. chopped onion
1 large garlic clove, minced
2 c. tomato sauce
¼ c. red wine vinegar
1 T. honey
2 T. capers, drained
⅔ c. stuffed olives, drained
    Freshly ground black pepper
    Salt

Heat oil over medium heat in a large skillet; sauté eggplant until golden and tender. Remove with slotted spoon. Add more oil if necessary. Stir in celery, onion, and garlic and sauté until tender and golden. Stir in tomato sauce and eggplant. Simmer, covered, for 10 minutes. Add remaining ingredients, except salt. Simmer, covered, 15 minutes or until mixture is thick and well done. Stir occasionally. Taste, add salt, and correct seasonings. Cool and then chill, covered, at least 4 hours, preferably overnight. Can be frozen or kept for several days in the refrigerator. Serve cold with toast rounds, crusty bread, or crisp crackers.

RYE BREAD STICKS

Yield: 4 dozen

2 pkgs. active dry yeast
2½ c. warm water
¼ c. brown sugar, well-packed
½ c. soft margarine
1 t. salt
4 c. sifted medium rye flour
2 T. caraway seed
4 c. whole wheat flour (approximately)
1 egg yolk beaten with 1 T. milk
    Caraway seed

Sprinkle yeast on warm water in a large mixing bowl; add brown sugar and stir until yeast is dissolved. Add all ingredients except whole wheat flour and egg yolk mixture and beat until smooth. Cover and let rise in a warm place (85°) about 45 minutes. Stir in whole wheat flour slowly; then turn dough out onto lightly floured board and knead until smooth (about 10 minutes). Divide dough into quarters; cut each quarter into 12 equal pieces. Shape each piece into a stick about 6 inches long. Place about 2 inches apart on greased baking sheets. Cover with towels and let rise in a warm place about 30 minutes or until doubled in bulk. Preheat oven to 400°. Brush sticks with egg yolk mixture and sprinkle with more caraway seeds as desired. Bake 15 minutes or until done. Remove from baking sheets and cool on wire racks. Store in airtight tins or freeze until needed.

Note: For thinner bread sticks, divide each quarter into more than 12 pieces. To make a rye "party loaf," divide the dough into fewer pieces. You must have similar sized "sticks" on the same baking sheet.

Soups and Stews

DIANE'S GAZPACHO

Yield: 8 to 10 servings

- 6 ripe tomatoes, blanched, peeled and chopped
- 1 large cucumber, deseeded, and chopped (peeled if necessary)
- 1 sweet green pepper, deseeded and chopped
- 1 sweet red pepper, deseeded and chopped
- ½ sweet onion, peeled and chopped
- 6 large garlic cloves, minced
- 1 small piece fresh chili pepper
- 1 c. (more or less to taste) tomato juice
- ½ c. olive or vegetable oil
- 2 t. salt
- Freshly grated black pepper

Thoroughly mix together all ingredients. Taste and correct seasonings. Serve ice cold.

WALKER-STALKER CREAM OF PARSLEY SOUP

Yield: 6 servings

- 2 c. chopped fresh parsley
- ½ c. chives (or onions), finely chopped
- ¼ c. butter or margarine
- 3 c. vegetable or garlic broth
- 1 c. water
- 2 T. whole wheat flour
- 2 c. milk
- ⅔ c. nonfat powdered milk
- ½ c. water
- Salt
- Freshly ground black pepper
- ⅔ c. freshly grated Parmesan cheese
- ⅔ c. grated Cheddar cheese
- Parsley

Place chives, parsley, butter, and broth in a large skillet or saucepan. Simmer until parsley is dark and limp (approximately 15 minutes). In a small bowl, stir water and flour together until a smooth paste is

*Photograph opposite:
Diane's Gazpacho*

formed. Add to cooked parsley and stir until smooth and thickened. Add milk and powdered milk and continue stirring until smooth. (Add more water if too thick.) Salt and pepper to taste. Approximately 5 minutes before serving, add cheeses. Cook until cheeses are melted. Correct seasonings. Garnish with fresh parsley, if desired.

LENTIL SOUP

Yield: 6 to 8 servings

- 1¾ c. dried lentils, washed, drained, and picked over
- 6 c. vegetable cooking liquid or broth
- 2 T. butter or margarine
- 1 c. chopped onion
- ½ c. chopped celery
- ⅔ c. chopped carrot
- ¼ lb. soy "bacon" bits (optional)
- 2 to 3 large cloves garlic, minced
- ¼ c. chopped parsley
- ½ t. thyme
- 1 bay leaf
- 1 T. butter
- Lemon juice
- Salt
- Freshly ground black pepper
- Optional garnishes: hard-boiled eggs, parsley, or sour cream

In a large kettle, bring lentils and broth to a boil. Cover and turn off heat. Melt 2 tablespoons butter in a large frying pan and add onion, celery, carrot, "bacon" bits, garlic, parsley, thyme, and bay leaf. Cover and let simmer over low heat approximately 10 minutes. Add the vegetables to the lentil mixture and simmer covered for 1½ hours. Put mixture through a food mill or blender. Heat to serving temperature and stir in 1 tablespoon butter. Add lemon juice, salt, and pepper to taste. Garnish as desired.

FRENCH TOMATO SOUP

Yield: 4 to 6 servings

- 1 T. butter or margarine
- 2 c. chopped onion
- 2 T. soy "bacon" bits
- 5 to 6 ripe tomatoes, chopped
- 1 strip lemon peel
- 4 c. Vegetable or Garlic Broth (p. 12, 15)
- ¼ c. chopped parsley
- 1 sprig thyme *or* ⅛ t. dry thyme
- 2 basil leaves *or* ½ t. dry basil
  Salt
  Freshly ground black pepper
  Parsley and basil, chopped
  Whole wheat garlic croutons

In a very large frying pan, melt butter. Add onion and sauté 5 to 6 minutes or until tender. Add "bacon" bits, tomatoes, peel, broth, and herbs. Bring to a boil; cover, lower heat, and simmer for about 20 minutes or until tender. Put soup through blender, if small bits of tomato skin remain, through a sieve. Add salt and pepper to taste. Serve hot; garnish with parsley, basil, and croutons.

GARLIC BROTH

Yield: 6 to 8 servings

- 14 to 16 garlic cloves, peeled and chopped
- 2 qts. water or vegetable cooking liquid
- 2 whole cloves
- ½ bay leaf
- 2 T. minced parsley
- 1 leaf sage *or* ¼ t. dried sage
- ½ t. thyme *or* ¼ t. dried thyme
  Freshly ground black pepper
  Salt
- ⅔ c. grated Swiss, Parmesan or Romano cheese
  Whole wheat bread rounds, toasted until dry

Place garlic, water, and next 5 ingredients into a large soup kettle; bring to a boil. Cover, lower heat, and let simmer for 30 minutes or until garlic is tender. Add pepper and salt to taste. Serve hot, garnished with toasted whole wheat bread rounds and grated cheese, or use this broth as the basis for other soups.

COLD LENTIL SOUP

Yield: 4 servings

- 1 c. chopped onion
- 2 T. vegetable oil
- ½ c. lentils, rounded
- 2½ c. Vegetable Broth (p. 15)
- 1 t. ground coriander
  Freshly ground black pepper
  Salt
- ½ c. chopped chive

Sauté onion in vegetable oil in a large frying pan or heavy bottomed pan. Stir in lentils; coat well with oil. Pour in Vegetable Broth; add coriander. Bring to a boil, turn down heat and let simmer, covered, for 1½ hours or until lentils are very tender. Add salt and pepper to taste during the last minutes of cooking. Put lentil mixture in blender or through sieve. When mixture is smooth, chill thoroughly. Serve very cold, garnished with chives.

BEAN AND SPLIT PEA SOUP

Yield: 6 to 8 servings

- 2 c. navy beans, soaked overnight in 7 c. water
- 1 c. dry white wine
- ½ c. chopped celery
- 1 c. chopped onion
- ½ c. sliced carrot
- ¼ c. chopped parsley
- 2 large garlic cloves, chopped
- 1 whole clove
- 2 bay leaves
- ½ t. thyme
- ¼ t. ground allspice
- 1 c. green split peas
- 1 T. lemon juice
  Freshly ground black pepper
  Salt

Bring beans and soaking liquid to a boil in a large soup kettle (not aluminum). Add all the rest of the ingredients except lemon juice, pepper, and salt. Simmer 1½ hours; then add lemon juice, and salt and pepper to taste. Continue cooking until beans are tender. (If you do not wish to have the split peas disintegrate into the stock, put them into soup during the last hour of cooking.)

MINESTRONE

Yield: 8 ample servings

2 qts. water or vegetable cooking liquid
10 to 12 large garlic cloves, peeled and chopped
1 c. chopped onion
2 whole cloves
1 leaf sage *or* ¼ t. dried sage
½ t. thyme *or* ¼ t. dried thyme
½ bay leaf
6 parsley sprigs
¼ t. oregano *or* ⅛ t. dried oregano
2 t. basil *or* 1 t. dried basil
2 c. cubed potato
2 c. sliced carrot
6 ripe tomatoes, cut into sixths, *or*
    3 c. canned tomatoes with juice
2 c. sliced zucchini
½ c. whole wheat shell macaroni
⅔ c. cooked kidney beans
    Freshly ground black pepper
    Salt
    Freshly grated Parmesan or Romano cheese

Heat water to boiling; add garlic cloves, onion, and seasonings except salt and pepper. Lower heat and let simmer for 30 minutes. Add potatoes, carrots, and ripe tomatoes, and simmer 15 minutes. Add zucchini, macaroni, and canned tomatoes; simmer until macaroni is just tender (15 to 20 minutes). Add kidney beans and heat thoroughly. Taste and add salt and pepper as desired. Serve immediately and garnish with Parmesan or Romano cheese.

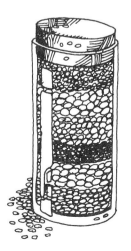

GREEK CABBAGE SOUP

Yield: 8 to 10 ample servings

1 T. olive oil
1 c. chopped onion
1 to 2 large garlic cloves, chopped
2 qts. water or vegetable cooking liquid
1 bay leaf
1 lb. tomatoes, chopped, *or*
    2 c. canned tomatoes and juice
2 lbs. cabbage, shredded
½ t. freshly ground black pepper
1½ t. salt
2 T. minced parsley

Sauté the onion and garlic in oil in a Dutch oven for about 5 minutes. Add water and bring to a boil. Lower heat, add bay leaf, tomatoes, and cabbage. Simmer until cabbage is tender (45 minutes or more, as desired). Add salt and pepper in the last minutes of cooking. Serve hot; garnish with parsley.

RED AND BLACK-EYED BEAN SOUP

Yield: 6 servings

6 c. water or vegetable cooking liquid
1 c. dried kidney beans
½ c. dried black-eyed peas
2 c. sliced onion
2 garlic cloves, minced
½ t. thyme
½ t. marjoram
1 c. cubed potato
1 c. sliced carrot
1 c. sliced celery
    Freshly ground black pepper
    Salt

Boil water in a large, heavy bottomed kettle; drop in kidney beans and black-eyed peas; let boil 2 minutes. Cover, turn off heat, and let stand for two hours. Stir in onion, garlic, thyme, and marjoram, and let simmer 1½ to 2 hours or until beans are just tender. Add potato, carrot, and celery (and tomato juice or more water if soup is too thick), and cook about 30 more minutes or until vegetables are tender. The last minutes of cooking, add salt and pepper to taste.

MOM'S VEGETABLE STEW

Yield: 3½ quarts

2½ qts. water
2 c. diced carrot
1 c. diced potato
1 c. sliced onion
1½ c. fresh or frozen green beans, cut
3 or 4 garlic cloves, minced
1 fresh or ½ c. canned tomato, chopped
3 T. fresh basil, chopped, or 1 T. dried basil
   Freshly ground black pepper
1 to 2 t. salt
½ c. whole wheat spaghetti, broken, or elbow macaroni
1 c. pimiento-stuffed olives, halved
2 c. cooked kidney beans
½ c. freshly grated Parmesan cheese

Bring water to boil in a large soup kettle; add next eight ingredients. Lower heat, cover and cook 10 to 15 minutes or until vegetables are just tender. Stir in salt, spaghetti, and olives. Cook until spaghetti is just barely tender, stirring occasionally. Add kidney beans and heat until piping hot. Correct seasonings. Serve immediately and garnish with Parmesan cheese.

FAMOUS RECIPE VEGETABLE SOUP

Yield: 8 servings

8 c. water or vegetable cooking liquid
½ c. dried yellow split peas
½ c. dried green split peas
½ c. dried barley
½ c. dried baby lima beans
1 bay leaf
1 whole clove
4 large garlic cloves, minced
1 c. chopped onion
2 T. minced parsley
2 c. sliced fresh or frozen green beans
1 c. sliced carrot
   Freshly ground black pepper
   Salt
½ c. whole wheat egg noodles, pasta, or alphabet noodles

Photograph opposite:
Mom's Vegetable Stew

Heat water to boiling in a large, heavy soup kettle. Meanwhile, rinse and pick over dried legumes. Add all the ingredients except salt and noodles; turn down heat, simmer, covered, stirring occasionally. Add more water if you desire a thinner soup. When the soup has simmered an hour, taste; add salt as desired, then stir in noodles. Continue to simmer until ingredients are tender, 15 to 30 minutes longer. Taste and correct seasonings.

Note: Add chopped celery ribs, fresh or dried mushrooms, chopped potatoes, leeks, tomatoes, or whatever you have on hand.

VEGETABLE BROTH

Yield: About 2 quarts

2 T. margarine or vegetable oil
1 c. chopped onion
2 to 3 large garlic cloves, chopped
2 qts. water or vegetable cooking liquid
1 c. sliced carrot
1 c. chopped celery
½ c. chopped turnip (optional)
½ c. chopped parsnips
1 c. shredded lettuce, chard, collards, or other greens
4 sprigs parsley
½ bay leaf
½ t. thyme
¼ t. marjoram
⅛ t. white pepper
⅛ t. cayenne
   Salt

Heat margarine in a Dutch oven; add onion and garlic and sauté about 5 minutes. Add water, bring to boil; lower heat and add all the ingredients except salt. Let simmer 1½ hours; taste, add salt, correct seasonings, and continue cooking up to one half hour more or until all the ingredients are very tender. Strain the broth and use it as the basis for other soups or dishes. (Strained broth can be frozen for later use.)

Note: You can add any other vegetables or their parings to this broth—potato skins, green peppers, leeks—whatever you have on hand will add to the flavor.

CAROLYN'S SCANDINAVIAN FRUIT SOUP

Yield: 10 to 12 servings

½ lb. raisins
½ c. dried apricots, well-packed
½ lb. pitted prunes
3 qts. water
2 apples, sliced
1 orange, sliced
1 stick of cinnamon
1 1-lb. can dark, pitted cherries (including juice)
1 c. canned peaches with juice
Any other fruits or juices on hand
2 to 3 T. tapioca

Soak raisins, apricots, and prunes in water overnight; pour into heavy-bottomed cooking pan. Add remaining ingredients and simmer, covered, 1½ hours or until well-flavored. Chill and serve cold. Can be made several days in advance and kept refrigerated until serving time.

BLACK BEAN SOUP

Yield: 6 servings

3 T. margarine or butter
1 c. chopped onion
4 garlic cloves
6 c. water or vegetable cooking liquid
½ c. chopped celery (with leaves)
6 sprigs parsley
½ c. chopped carrot
1 bay leaf
Freshly ground black pepper
Salt

Melt margarine in a heavy soup kettle or Dutch oven. Add onion and garlic; sauté until onion is transparent. Stir in rest of ingredients in order except salt. Add salt the last 30 minutes of cooking. Cook 2 to 3 hours or until beans are tender (depends upon type and age of black beans). Put through sieve or blend in blender, if desired. Heat to serve and garnish with hard-boiled egg slices, soy "bacon" bits, or minced onion.

AVGOLEMONO SOUP
(Greek egg and lemon soup)

Yield: 8 servings

8 c. well-flavored Vegetable Broth (p. 15)
1¼ c. brown rice, washed and picked over
Freshly ground black pepper
Salt
2 whole eggs
2 to 4 T. fresh lemon juice
4 T. chopped parsley or chives

Bring vegetable broth to a boil; add rice, cover and simmer until rice is tender (45 to 50 minutes). Taste; add pepper and salt; remove from heat. Beat eggs well and add lemon juice; continue beating. Take a ladleful of soup; stir it into the egg mixture. Beat thoroughly. Pour the egg mixture into the soup slowly, stirring constantly. Reheat soup and cook until it thickens. *Do not let the soup boil or the eggs will curdle.* Taste and correct seasonings. Garnish with parsley or chives and serve immediately.

CARROT SOUP

Yield: 8 servings

3 T. margarine or butter
4 c. sliced carrot
1 c. sliced onion
⅛ t. thyme
8 c. Vegetable or Garlic Broth (p. 12, 15)
⅓ c. brown rice
Salt
Freshly ground black pepper
2 T. thinly sliced margarine or butter

Melt 3 tablespoons margarine in a large, heavy bottomed pan or Dutch oven over low heat. Stir in carrot, onion, thyme, and pepper. Cover and let cook about 10 minutes, stirring occasionally. Add broth; simmer mixture and add rice. Let cook until rice is tender (45 to 50 minutes). Put mixture in blender or through a sieve. When mixture is smooth, add salt and pepper to taste. Bring the soup to serving temperature, stir in 2 tablespoons butter and serve immediately.

Sandwiches

TOFU, OLIVE, AND SPROUT SANDWICHES

Yield: 4 sandwiches

1 c. tofu
1 small garlic clove, minced
3 T. raw wheat germ
3 green onions, chopped
1 rib celery, chopped
¾ t. minced fresh basil
¾ t. minced fresh rosemary
½ t. minced fresh fennel
¾ t. minced fresh oregano
1 T. mayonnaise
8 pimiento stuffed olives, chopped
   Dash of freshly ground black pepper
8 slices bread or toast
   Margarine or butter
½ t. chili powder (optional)
1 c. alfalfa sprouts, packed down

Mash tofu and mix in remaining ingredients in order up to bread. When thoroughly blended, taste and correct seasonings. Butter 4 slices of bread, sprinkle with chili powder, if desired. Divide spread among unbuttered bread slices; top with alfalfa sprouts, and assemble sandwiches.

LENTIL TOSTADAS

Yield: 6 servings

1½ c. dried lentils, washed and sorted
3 c. water or vegetable cooking liquid
1 bay leaf
½ c. chopped onion
1 small whole clove
1 T. chopped parsley
⅛ t. dried thyme
1 large garlic clove, minced
1½ t. chili powder
⅛ t. ground cumin

   Dash of freshly ground black pepper
   Salt
6 tortillas

In a large, heavy kettle combine all ingredients except salt and tortillas. Cover and quickly bring to a boil. Reduce heat; simmer, covered, until lentils are tender, approximately 1 hour. Remove clove and bay leaf and mash lentil mixture thoroughly by hand or in blender. When completely blended, taste and correct seasonings. Sauté tortillas briefly in a small amount of oil; drain on paper towels or heat in oven. Keep warm until ready to serve. Top with lentil mixture; garnish as desired.
Note: May garnish with shredded lettuce or spinach; chopped tomato, chopped chive or green onion; Guacamole, or avocado slices, and grated Cheddar cheese or yogurt.

CAROLYN'S GOLDEN TEMPLE SANDWICH

Yield: 4 open-faced sandwiches

4 slices bread, toasted on one side
4 large slices Mozzarella, sharp Cheddar, Muenster, or other cheese
   Minced onion
½ c. sliced fresh mushroom
½ c. chopped tomato
   Guacamole (p. 4)
1 to 2 c. alfalfa sprouts

Layer cheese slices on untoasted side of bread; add onion to taste, mushroom, and tomato. Place under broiler and grill until cheese melts. Immediately top with Guacamole and alfalfa sprouts. Serve.

BEAN TOSTADA

Yield: 6 servings

- 4 c. water or vegetable cooking liquid
- 2 c. dry pinto beans
- 2 c. chopped onion
- 2 garlic cloves, minced
- 1 yellow hot pepper or 2 small green, chopped
- ½ t. crushed hot red peppers (dry)
- ½ t. sweet red pepper flakes
- 4 T. fresh oregano or 2 T. dried
- 1 T. ground coriander seed
- 1 T. cumin seed
- 1 t. paprika
- ⅛ t. cayenne pepper
- 4 large ripe tomatoes, chopped or 2 c. canned tomato
  Dash of freshly ground black pepper
- 1½ t. salt
- 6 stone ground corn tortillas

Bring water to boil; add beans, cover and cook for two minutes. Turn off heat and let stand for two hours. Add remaining ingredients except salt and simmer 2 to 3 hours or until beans are tender. Add salt the last 15 to 20 minutes. Taste and correct seasonings. Just before serving, heat tortillas in oven or sauté briefly in a small amount of oil and drain on paper towels. Keep warm until ready to serve. Spoon bean mixture on top of tortillas. Garnish with shredded lettuce, chopped tomatoes, grated Cheddar or Monterey Jack cheese or yogurt.
Note: Use as pita filling or on whole wheat bread or toast.

VEGETARIAN SUBMARINE

Yield: 1 large submarine sandwich

- 1 large whole wheat submarine sandwich roll, sliced lengthwise
- 3 to 4 large cheese slices
- ¾ c. hot, sautéed mushroom and onion
  Shredded lettuce
- 1 tomato, sliced
  Pickle and raw onion slices, if desired

Place cheese on bottom half of roll and place under broiler until cheese melts. Top with sautéed mushroom and onion, lettuce, tomato slices, pickles, and raw onion. Replace top of roll; slice into individual servings. (May broil top part of roll in aluminum foil while melting cheese on bottom half.) Serve hot.

AVOCADO 'N EGG SANDWICHES

Yield: 4 sandwiches

- 8 thin slices whole wheat bread
  Butter or margarine
- 1 ripe avocado
- 4 hard-boiled eggs, chilled
- ½ c. mayonnaise, chilled
  Dash of freshly ground black pepper
  Dash of salt
  Crisp lettuce

Spread small amount of butter on bread slices. With a fork or pastry blender, mash eggs and avocado together. Add mayonnaise and pepper. Taste and add salt. (If making ahead, add lemon juice to prevent avocado from discoloring.) Spread mixture on half the buttered bread; add lettuce and assemble sandwiches.
Note: Alfalfa sprouts may be substituted for the lettuce.

TOFU SALAD SANDWICH

Yield: 4 sandwiches

- 1 c. tofu
- 1 small garlic clove, minced
- 3 T. raw wheat germ
- 1 T. chopped parsley
- ¼ t. turmeric
- ¼ t. dry mustard
- ¼ t. celery seed
- ½ t. chopped fresh oregano
- ½ t. chopped sweet basil
- ½ t. crushed dill weed
- 1 T. mayonnaise
- 4 green onions, chopped
- 2 ribs celery, chopped
- ¼ t. paprika
  Dash of freshly ground black pepper
  Dash of salt
- 8 slices toast or bread
  Margarine or butter
- 1 c. alfalfa sprouts, packed down

Mash tofu thoroughly. Mix in remaining ingredients in order up to the bread, until spread is well-blended. Taste and correct seasonings. May be chilled until serving time. Butter four slices of toast; spread tofu mixture on unbuttered slices; top with alfalfa sprouts. Assemble sandwiches.

Photograph opposite:
Bean Tostada

Breads and Breakfasts

SIX-LOAVES-AT-A-TIME PROTEIN BREAD

Yield: Six 1½-pound loaves

- 6 pkgs. dry yeast
- 6 c. lukewarm milk
- ¾ c. honey
- 3 eggs, beaten
- ¾ c. soy flour, sifted
- 2 c. non-instant powdered milk
- ¾ c. raw wheat germ
- ⅓ c. nutritional yeast
- 2 T. salt
- 12 to 15 c. (nearly 4 lbs.) whole wheat flour or graham flour
  Vegetable oil

In a very large container, mix together yeast, milk, and honey. Let stand in a warm place for 5 minutes. Stir in eggs and remaining ingredients, adding only 3 cups of whole wheat flour at this time. Beat thoroughly. Stir in additional flour until a soft dough is formed. Turn dough out onto a well-floured, large surface, and knead until smooth (this may take up to 15 minutes). Place dough in a large, well-greased container. Cover with damp towel and let rise in a warm place (85°) until doubled in bulk, one hour or more. Punch down, let rest for 10 minutes, covered. Divide dough into six loaves and place in well-greased tins, large juice or coffee cans, or directly on baking sheets. Cover loaves with damp towels and let rise again in a warm place about 45 minutes or until doubled in bulk. Bake in a 350° oven 45 minutes to 1 hour, or until done. Remove immediately from pans and place on wire racks to cool. Brush top crust with butter if softer crust is desired.

PITA OR POCKET BREAD

Make above recipe. Take out as much dough as you like, divide it into balls approximately 2 inches in diameter. On a lightly floured surface, roll out each ball with a lightly floured rolling pin, forming rounds about ¼ inch thick. Sprinkle lightly with flour, cover with a cloth, let rise. Preheat oven to 450°. Lightly oil baking sheets as needed and place in oven to heat. When bread rounds have risen, slip them gently onto baking sheets, sprinkle tops with cold water, and bake for 6 to 10 minutes. Bread is done if it sounds hollow when tapped. Remove from baking sheets immediately and place on wire racks to cool.

DINNER ROLLS

From Six-Loaves-At-A-Time dough, set aside desired amount of dough, roll out about 1/3 inch thick, and brush with melted butter. Cut out with round cutter. Crease center with a knife. Fold in half, place on greased baking sheet and let rise. Bake in a 350° oven for about 20 minutes. "Cloverleaf" rolls can be made by dividing desired amount of dough into small balls and placing 3 or 4 balls in each cup of well-greased muffin tins. Let rise and bake in a 350° oven for about 20 minutes.

PIZZA

Make Six-Loaves-At-A-Time recipe. After the dough has risen the first time, take out enough to spread onto a well-greased pizza pan or baking sheet. Brush top of the dough with vegetable oil. Fill as desired with your favorite tomato sauce (consider adding mashed tofu, soy "beef" bit, and/or minced onions and garlic to your sauce). Spread plenty of grated mozzarella or other cheese on top, add chopped green peppers, mushrooms, sliced olives, etc., and sprinkle oregano and/or freshly grated Parmesan cheese over the entire surface. Bake in a 425° oven for approximately 25 minutes or until done.

SOURDOUGH HI-PROTEIN BREAD

Yield: 2 Loaves
STARTER

2 c. lukewarm water
1 pkg. active dry yeast
2 c. whole wheat flour

Place water in a glass mixing bowl. Sprinkle with yeast and stir with a wooden spoon until yeast is dissolved. Add flour and beat until smooth. Cover with a towel and let stand in a warm place (85°) for 48 hours. Stir once or twice a day with a wooden spoon. Remove enough dough for the recipe; stir equal amounts of flour and water (usually 1 cup flour and 1 cup lukewarm water) into the starter. Let ferment about 5 hours, then cover and refrigerate in a clean, wide-mouthed glass container. (Do not put cover on tightly; the jar might crack during fermentation.) Used regularly and replenished about once a week, sourdough starter can be kept indefinitely. Separation of the starter is normal; just stir with a wooden spoon thoroughly before using.

This sourdough method allows you to let your starter grow. Every few days, let the mixture return to room temperature and add equal parts water and flour; let it ferment, then return to refrigerator. If you have a large amount of sourdough starter on hand, you can make double or even triple-sized recipes. For a different flavor, experiment with rye and oat flours.
Note: Always have starter at room temperature before using in a recipe.

SOURDOUGH BREAD

1¼ c. lukewarm milk
1 pkg. active dry yeast
3 T. honey
2 t. salt
1½ c. Sourdough Starter (at room temperature)
¼ c. soy flour, sifted
¼ c. nutritional yeast
¼ c. non-instant powdered milk
½ c. raw wheat germ
4½ c. (approximately) whole wheat flour

Pour milk into a large mixing bowl; sprinkle yeast on top. In order given, stir in remaining ingredients except whole wheat flour. When thoroughly mixed, add flour; dough will be soft. Cover with a cloth and let rise in a warm place (85°) for one hour or until doubled in bulk. Turn dough out on heavily floured surface and knead 10 minutes or until smooth, adding flour as necessary. Shape into loaves and place in two well-greased 9 x 5-inch loaf tins. Cover and allow to rise again in a warm place 45 minutes or until almost doubled in size. Place loaves in a 450° oven and bake 35 minutes or until done. Remove bread from tins to cool on wire racks. Brush tops of loaves with butter if soft crust is desired.
Note: This recipe can be used to make pita bread or dinner rolls; see variations under "Six-Loaves-At-A-Time Protein Bread."

BAKED WHOLE WHEAT DOUGHNUTS

Yield: 2 dozen or more

2 pkgs. active dry yeast
¼ c. lukewarm water
1½ c. lukewarm milk
⅓ c. honey
¼ t. cinnamon
1 t. nutmeg
1 t. salt
2 eggs
½ c. shortening or margarine
¼ c. soy flour
1 T. nutritional yeast
¼ c. wheat germ
4 to 5 c. whole wheat flour
Melted butter or margarine

In a large mixing bowl, dissolve yeast in warm water. Add milk, honey, spices, salt, eggs, shortening, soy flour, yeast, wheat germ, and 1½ cups of the flour. Blend 30 seconds on low speed, scraping bowl constantly. Beat 2 minutes at medium speed. Stir in remaining flour until soft dough is formed. When well mixed, cover; let rise in a warm place until double, 50 to 60 minutes. Turn dough out onto well-floured, cloth-covered board. Roll gently with well-floured rolling pin until dough is ½ inch thick. Cut with floured doughnut cutter. Put leftover scraps together and continue making doughnuts until all dough has been used. Place doughnuts on well-greased baking tins, brush with melted butter. Cover. Let rise in a warm place about 20 minutes or until double. Preheat oven to 425°. Bake 8 to 10 minutes or until golden. Immediately brush with melted butter and shake in brown cinnamon sugar or icing sugar or serve plain.

PARATHA

Yield: 8 to 10 parathas

Fried, whole wheat bread from India

- 2 c. whole wheat flour
- ½ t. salt
- 2 T. ghee (clarified butter)*
  Cold water
  Additional melted ghee

Sift the flour and salt together into a large mixing bowl. Work in the butter with fingertips until mixture resembles coarse meal. Pour ⅓ cup water over the mixture; mix well. Add more water slowly until a workable dough is formed. Knead well on a lightly floured surface (10 to 15 minutes). Gather dough up into a ball, place in a bowl and cover. Set aside 1 hour. Knead again. Shape into 8 to 10 balls. Roll each ball into a 6 or 7-inch round. Brush top lightly with melted ghee. Fold round in half and brush again. Fold once more into a rough triangle shape, roll lightly with rolling pin. (You can set them aside up to 4 hours at room temperature, covered with a damp towel, before frying.) Heat a large griddle or skillet and lightly brush with ghee. Fry parathas on both sides, continously brushing with butter, until golden, crisp, and flaky. Serve warm as they are or make a sandwich with them. They may be cooked ahead and reheated in an ungreased pan for a short time on each side.

*To clarify butter (ghee), melt butter in a saucepan over medium heat, skimming off foam constantly. Remove from heat and strain the clear liquid. Discard the residue in the bottom of the pan. Can be made ahead and stored in the refrigerator.

DATE NUT BREAD

Yield: 1 loaf

- 1¼ c. boiling water
- 2 c. cut-up dates
- ½ c. old-fashioned molasses
- ⅓ c. honey
- 1 T. melted butter
- 1 egg
- 1 t. vanilla
- 2½ t. baking powder
- 2¾ c. whole wheat pastry flour
- ½ t. salt
- ¼ c. raw wheat germ
- ¼ c. non-instant powdered milk
- 1 c. chopped nuts

Mix boiling water and dates together in a large mixing bowl; let stand until lukewarm. Preheat oven to 350°. Add molasses, honey, butter, egg, and vanilla to dates. In a separate bowl, mix all dry ingredients except nuts. Combine with date mixture and blend thoroughly. Stir in nuts. Pour into greased bread pan and bake for about an hour or until top springs back when lightly pressed.

WHOLE WHEAT CRUMPETS

Yield: 12 crumpets

- ½ c. milk
- ½ c. boiling water
- 1 ⅝-oz. cake yeast
- 1 t. honey
- ¾ t. salt
- 1¾ c. sifted whole wheat pastry flour
- 2 t. baking powder
- 3 T. hot tap water
- ½ c. raisins or chopped apples (optional)
- ½ t. cinnamon (optional)
- 4 or more tuna fish (or similar type) cans with tops and bottoms removed, and washed well

Mix milk and boiling water together in a large mixing bowl. Cool to lukewarm (90°). Stir in yeast and honey and let stand in warm place for 10 minutes. Stir in salt and flour. Mix well, cover with a towel, and let rise in a warm place (84° - 86°) until very bubbly and almost doubled in bulk (about 30 to 40 minutes). Mix baking powder with the hot tap water. Stir into batter and let rise again, covered, in a warm place until doubled in bulk (about 30 minutes).

Heat a lightly greased griddle or very large skillet until a drop of water jumps when sprinkled on it. Place as many lightly greased tuna fish can rings on the griddle as you have and spread small amount of batter evenly into the bottom of them. Cook *slowly* until brown on bottom and dry on top. Remove rings. Turn and let brown quickly on the other side. Repeat until all batter is used up. To serve, split with a fork; then toast. (For best results place under broiler, uncooked sides up.) Eat while hot.

Photograph opposite: Date Nut Bread

MRS. ROGERS' OATMEAL BREAD

Yield: 3 loaves

2 c. rolled oats
4 c. boiling water
1 c. sorghum or molasses
1 T. margarine
1 T. salt
1 pkg. dry yeast
¾ c. warm water
1 T. honey
1 c. raw wheat germ
½ c. soy flour, sifted
7 c. (approximately) whole wheat flour
½ c. bran
¼ c. nutritional yeast

Place oats in a large bowl; pour boiling water over and add sorghum, margarine, and salt. Set aside to cool. In a small bowl, combine yeast, warm water, and honey. When oat mixture is cool, stir in wheat germ, flours, bran, nutritional yeast, and yeast mixture; blend thoroughly. Dough will be soft. Cover with a towel and place in a warm place overnight. The next morning, stir the dough down. Place on a well-floured surface, adding flour as necessary, and knead ten minutes or until smooth. Form dough into 3 loaves on a well-floured surface and place into three well-greased 8½ x 4½ x 2⅝-inch loaf pans. Let rise again. Bake 35 minutes in a 350° oven. Remove immediately and cool on wire racks.

RYE POPOVERS

Yield: 1 dozen

¾ c. medium rye flour
¾ c. whole wheat pastry flour
¼ t. salt
2 eggs, well beaten
1 c. milk

Preheat oven to 450°. Sift dry ingredients together. Add eggs and milk to the flour mixture and make a smooth batter. Beat with electric mixer until batter is full of air bubbles. Meanwhile, grease two 6-cup muffin tins and place into oven to heat. Fill each cup 2/3 full. Bake 15 minutes; reduce heat to 350° and bake an additional 15 minutes until popovers are golden.
Note: If you wish a higher popover, substitute unbleached flour for the whole wheat flour.

GRANOLA

Yield: 9 to 10 cups

6 c. rolled oats
½ c. bran
2 c. raw wheat germ
1½ c. raw nuts and/or ground roasted, unsalted soybeans
¼ c. sesame seeds
½ c. soy flour, sifted
¼ c. nutritional yeast
½ c. honey
½ c. vegetable oil
1 t. salt
1 c. raisins
1 c. unsalted, roasted sunflower seeds

Preheat oven to 275°. Combine all ingredients except raisins and sunflower seeds; mix well. Spread evenly and not too thickly on two large baking sheets. Bake until golden (about 45 minutes), stirring approximately every 15 minutes. When cool, add raisins, seeds, and any optional ingredients of your choice. Store in tightly covered container in the refrigerator. Serve as a breakfast cereal with milk, yogurt, fruit, etc. or as an ingredient in cookies, breads, or snack items.

APRICOT-NUT BREAD

Yield: 1 loaf

1½ c. unbleached flour
1½ c. whole wheat flour
1 T. baking powder
¼ t. baking soda
1 t. salt
¼ c. margarine
1 c. milk
½ c. honey
¼ c. brown sugar
½ c. chopped walnuts
½ c. chopped dried apricots
2 T. raw wheat germ
2 T. chopped walnuts

Preheat oven to 350°. Sift dry ingredients together into a large mixing bowl. Melt margarine. Cool slightly and add milk, honey, and sugar. Stir milk mixture into dry ingredients. Stir ½ cup nuts and apricots into the batter. Spoon batter into a well-greased 9 x 5 x 3-inch loaf pan. Sprinkle wheat germ on top, then sprinkle with nuts. Bake for about an hour or until a toothpick inserted in the middle comes out clean. Let cool about 10 minutes before removing from pan. Finish cooling on wire rack.

WHOLE WHEAT BLINTZES

Yield: 6 to 8 servings

    3 eggs
    1 c. whole wheat pastry flour, sifted
    ¼ c. non-instant powdered milk
    ¼ c. raw wheat germ
    1¼ c. milk
    3 T. vegetable oil
      Fresh strawberry sauce, bananas,
      yogurt, blueberries, etc. for topping

In a medium bowl, beat eggs lightly; mix dry ingredients together and combine with eggs until just blended. Add milk and oil. Cover and let rest in refrigerator for 45 minutes to one hour.

Heat a crepe pan or other 6 to 8-inch skillet. When a drop of water sprinkled onto pan bounces, grease lightly with small amount of butter. Pour small amount of batter into pan, moving it from side to side to cover bottom. Cook on only one side until top is set and underside is done. Drain on toweling and continue process until all batter is used.

Divide Filling among blintzes, placing in center of the browned side of the blintz. Fold blintz similarly to an envelope. Fold two opposite sides over filling, fold one end up and the other end down over all. In a large skillet, melt small amount of butter. Cook blintzes until golden with the folded side down, turn to brown the other side. Add more butter as needed. Keep warm until all are cooked. Serve immediately with desired topping.

FILLING

    2 c. cottage cheese, drained dry
    1 egg
    2 T. honey
    ½ t. vanilla

In a large bowl mix together cottage cheese, egg, honey, and vanilla. Beat with an electric beater at high speed until smooth.

MIXED GRAIN CEREAL

Yield: Approximately 3¾ lbs.

    1 lb. rolled oats
    1 lb. flaked or rolled wheat
    1 lb. rolled rye
    ½ lb. raw or toasted wheat germ
    ¼ lb. bran

Mix all ingredients together thoroughly and store in a tightly covered tin. Use as a breakfast cereal, adding raw or dried fruit, milk, honey, and/or yogurt; or use in cookie recipes that call for oatmeal.

Note: Nuts and any other grain that appeals to you can be added to or substituted for the above.

CELESTE'S CHEESE AND BEER BREAD

Yield: 2 loaves

    1½ c. beer
    ⅔ c. water or vegetable cooking liquid
    ½ c. vegetable oil
    6 c. (approximately) whole wheat flour or graham flour
    ½ c. brown sugar, well-packed
    ½ c. raw wheat germ
    2 t. salt
    2 pkgs. active dry yeast
    1 egg
    2 c. grated sharp Cheddar cheese

Heat beer, water, and oil in a small pan until very warm (about 120°). In a large bowl, combine beer mixture, 2½ cups flour, and remaining ingredients, except cheese. Beat thoroughly with electric mixer for about 2 minutes at medium speed. With a wooden spoon, stir in remaining flour until soft dough is formed. Turn out onto well-floured surface; knead until smooth (about 10 minutes). Place in a greased bowl; turn once. Cover with a towel and let rise in a warm place (about 85°) until doubled in size (1 hour or more).

Line two 9 x 5-inch loaf tins with aluminum foil; grease thoroughly. When dough has risen, punch down, divide in half, and flatten each half on well-floured surface. Pour 1 cup Cheddar cheese into the center of each flattened surface and roll up carefully into well-shaped loaves. Place in prepared tins. Cover and let rise again until doubled in size (45 to 60 minutes). Preheat oven to 350°. Bake loaves 40 to 50 minutes or until done. Remove from tins immediately and place on wire racks to cool. If soft crusts are desired, brush with melted butter.

Note: If you desire higher loaves, substitute some unbleached flour for the whole wheat flour.

MOM'S BRAN MUFFINS

Yield: 12 muffins

1¼ c. bran
¼ c. raw wheat germ
1 c. whole wheat flour
½ c. raisins
½ t. salt
1 t. baking soda
1 t. baking powder
¾ c. milk
⅓ c. honey
2 T. vegetable oil
1 egg, beaten

Preheat oven to 400°. Stir together first 7 dry ingredients and set aside. Mix together milk, honey, oil and egg. Add to dry ingredients and stir just until moistened. Spoon into well-greased muffin cups or paper liners and bake about 15 minutes or until done.

MRS. SCHULKE'S BASIC BUCKWHEAT PANCAKE MIX

BASIC MIX

Yield: About 6 cups starter

1½ c. buckwheat flour
1½ c. whole wheat pastry flour
⅓ c. nutritious yeast
1 c. soy flour
3 T. baking powder
1¼ c. raw wheat germ
2 t. salt
½ c. non-instant powdered milk

Thoroughly mix together all ingredients. Store in freezer or refrigerator.
Note: Whole wheat pastry flour can be substituted for buckwheat flour.

BUCKWHEAT PANCAKES

Yield: 12 Pancakes

1¼ c. sweet or sour milk
1 egg
2 T. vegetable oil
1½ c. Mrs. Schulke's Basic Buckwheat Pancake Mix

Combine liquid ingredients and add to pancake mix, stirring only until ingredients are blended. Spoon onto a lightly greased, hot griddle.

Photograph opposite:
Mom's Bran Muffins

PRUNEOLA

Yield: About 3 pounds

6 c. rolled oats or a mixture of grains
1 c. raw wheat germ
½ c. sesame seeds
1 c. chopped nuts
1 c. raw sunflower seeds
½ c. vegetable oil
⅓ c. honey
12 oz. pitted prunes, chopped

Preheat oven to 300°. Combine first five ingredients in a large bowl. Mix honey and vegetable oil together in a small pan and heat until just below a boil. Stir oil mixture into dry ingredients. Spread mixture very thinly on two very large flat baking pans or cookie sheets. Bake, stirring occasionally, for 25 minutes or until mixture is golden. Remove from pans into a large bowl and immediately stir in prunes. Let cool. Store in large container with tight cover. Eat as a cereal with milk, fruit, nuts, or yogurt added.

ZUCCHINI-BRAN BREAD

Yield: One 9 x 5-inch loaf or
Two 7 x 4-inch loaves

¼ c. soy flour
2 T. nutritional yeast
1½ c. bran
2⅔ c. whole wheat flour
1 T. baking powder
½ t. baking soda
1 t. salt
1½ t. cinnamon
¼ t. ginger
¾ c. honey
⅓ c. vegetable oil
½ c. milk
2 eggs, beaten
2 c. grated zucchini
¼ c. chopped nuts
½ c. raisins

Preheat oven to 325°. Stir first 9 dry ingredients together. In a separate bowl, stir together honey, oil, milk, and eggs. Add honey mixture to dry ingredients; stir in zucchini, nuts, and raisins. Pour into well-greased 9 x 5-inch loaf pan or two 7 x 4-inch pans and bake 60 minutes or until golden (less time for smaller loaves). Cool 10 minutes in pan and then turn out onto wire racks to finish cooling.

Main Dishes

American

GARDEN HARVEST CASSEROLE

Yield: 6 to 8 servings

1 c. sliced and unpeeled eggplant
1 c. thinly sliced carrots
1 c. sliced green beans
1 c. diced potatoes
2 medium tomatoes, quartered
1 small yellow squash, sliced
1 small zucchini, sliced
1 medium onion, sliced
½ c. chopped green pepper
½ c. chopped cabbage
3 cloves garlic, crushed
3 sprigs parsley, chopped
　Freshly ground black pepper
1 c. beef bouillon
⅓ c. vegetable oil
2 t. salt
¼ t. tarragon
½ bay leaf, crumpled

Mix vegetables together and place into a shallow baking dish (13 x 9 x 2 inch). Sprinkle parsley and grind pepper over all. At this point you can refrigerate until ready to bake. Preheat oven to 350°. Pour bouillon into a small saucepan; add oil, salt, tarragon, and bay leaf. Heat to boiling; correct seasonings. Pour over vegetables. Cover baking dish with aluminium foil; bake 1 to 1½ hours or until vegetables are just tender and are still colorful. Carefully stir vegetables occasionally; but to preserve color, don't lift cover off for very long.

Note: You can substitute other vegetables if they are in harvest and they appeal to you.

JACKIE'S STUFFED ACORN SQUASH

Yield: 4 servings

2 acorn squash
　Butter
1½ c. frozen peas
½ c. grated sharp Cheddar cheese
　Salt to taste
　Freshly ground black pepper to taste

Slice squash in half lengthwise; remove seeds and membrane. Place squash, cut side down, in a baking pan. Add about ½ inch water and bake in a 350° oven 45 minutes to 1 hour. When squash is just tender, turn and butter the inside. Divide peas among squash, sprinkle cheese on top, and salt and pepper to taste. Add more water, if necessary; cover with aluminum foil and heat through. Serve hot.

Note: May also add steamed pearl onions to the dish or use mixed vegetables, creamed chard or spinach, or whatever vegetable appeals.

LAYERED DINNER

Yield: 6 to 8 servings

1 c. sliced carrot
1 c. sliced potatoes
1 c. sliced celery
¾ c. brown rice
　Salt to taste
　Freshly ground black pepper to taste
1 c. sliced onion
3 c. canned tomatoes and juice
½ c. raw wheat germ

Preheat oven to 350°. Place layers as listed into a buttered 2-quart casserole. Salt and pepper the rice layer as desired. Sprinkle wheat germ on top. Cover with a tight-fitting cover or heavy foil; bake 2 hours or until vegetables are tender and rice is done. Add more juice, if necessary. Remove cover the last 10 minutes of baking to toast top, if desired.

LOUISIANA RED BEANS AND RICE

Yield: 6 servings

8 c. water or vegetable cooking liquid
2 c. (1-lb.) dried red kidney beans, rinsed and sorted
4 large cloves garlic
1 c. chopped onion
¼ c. soy "bacon" bits (optional)
Freshly ground black pepper to taste
Salt to taste
2 c. cooked brown rice

In a heavy bottomed kettle soak beans in 5 cups water overnight. Add another 3 cups water and the remaining ingredients, except salt. (Or bring beans to a boil in 8 cups water; boil 2 minutes and turn off heat. Cover and let sit for 2 hours; then proceed with the recipe.) Simmer beans slowly 3 to 4 hours or until beans are very tender and a thick sauce has formed. Add salt to taste in the last 20 minutes of cooking. Serve over hot brown rice.

STUFFED GREEN PEPPERS

Yield: 8 servings

4 green peppers
1 T. vegetable oil
1½ c. chopped onion
1 clove garlic, chopped
2 large ripe tomatoes, chopped
1½ c. cooked brown rice
1 t. chili powder
Salt to taste
Freshly ground black pepper to taste
¾ c. grated sharp Cheddar cheese

Slice peppers in half; remove stalks and seeds. Steam until just tender. Sauté onion and garlic in oil until onion is translucent. Add tomatoes; heat until mixture is well blended and tender. Mix with rice. Add seasonings to taste. Preheat oven to 375°. Place peppers in a lightly greased baking dish. Spoon mixture into pepper cases, sprinkle grated cheese on top. Cover and bake for 30 minutes or until cheese melts. If desired, put dish under broiler for a few minutes to brown slightly. Serve hot.

French

MAKE-AHEAD SOUFFLÉ

Yield: 6 servings

1 T. butter
2 to 3 shallots *or* 1 T. minced onion
1½ c. chopped spinach, chard, or broccoli
1 T. lemon juice
6 large eggs, separated
6 T. butter or margarine
6 T. whole wheat flour
1 t. salt
Freshly ground black pepper
1½ c. milk
¼ c. instant powdered milk
Freshly grated Parmesan cheese

Melt butter in heavy saucepan and add minced shallots. Cook about 3 minutes, stirring once or twice. Add vegetables and lemon juice and cook over low heat, stirring frequently until liquid has evaporated (about 10 minutes). Set aside. In heavy saucepan (or over boiling water in the top part of a double boiler), melt butter and blend in flour and seasonings thoroughly. Add milks all at once and cook, stirring constantly with a wire whisk, until mixture is smooth and thickened. Remove from heat; beat egg yolks until thick. Slowly stir yolks into milk mixture; stir in vegetables and set aside. With clean, dry beaters, beat egg whites until stiff but not dry. (They should hold soft peaks.) Gradually stir yolk mixture into whites, folding carefully with rubber scraper until well-blended. Butter soufflé dish lightly and sprinkle with Parmesan cheese. At this point the soufflé can be refrigerated for up to 8 hours or even frozen, unbaked. Preheat oven to 350°. Bake the soufflé, uncovered, for 45 minutes, or until puffed and golden brown. (Do not open oven door until time is up.) Allow longer cooking time if frozen.

JENNIFER'S CARROT FLAN

Yield: 8 servings

1 Double Pastry Crust (p. 60) (made in a
   10-inch flan tin)
¾ lb. new carrots, scraped
1 to 3 T. honey
1 T. soft butter
1 2-inch piece of orange peel
3 eggs
1¼ c. carrot steaming liquid, cooled
½ c. non-instant powdered milk

Preheat oven to 400°. Place crust in oven for 10 minutes, prick bottom if bubbles form. When crust firms, remove from oven. Reduce heat to 375°. Meanwhile, using a steamer-rack and 2 cups water, steam carrots until tender. Put steamed carrots in blender; add remaining ingredients and blend until smooth. Taste and correct seasonings. Pour carrot mixture into flan crust; bake until just firm (30 to 40 minutes). Serve warm.

SPINACH-ONION-MUSHROOM CREPES

Yield: 10 crepes

2 T. butter or margarine
¾ c. chopped onion
1 8-oz. can mushrooms, sliced
1 10-oz. pkg. chopped spinach, steamed
2 c. milk
¼ t. salt
¼ c. non-instant powdered milk
2 T. butter
3 T. whole wheat flour
1 4-oz. pkg. Swiss cheese, grated
¼ c. raw wheat germ
⅓ c. Parmesan cheese
10 Whole Wheat Crepes (p. 33)

Sauté onion and mushrooms in butter until onion is tender. Stir in steamed spinach; make certain all liquid in the pan has evaporated. Turn off heat. Mix together milk, salt, and non-instant powdered milk in a heavy-bottomed saucepan. Heat almost to a boil. Meanwhile, melt butter in a heavy skillet, stir in flour, and cook for about 2 minutes, stirring constantly. Do not allow mixture to scorch. Add hot milk all at once; continue stirring with a wire whisk until sauce comes to a boil. Boil for about 1 minute, stirring constantly. Remove from heat, taste and correct seasonings. Stir in Swiss cheese. Add ½ cup of Swiss cheese sauce into onion/spinach mixture stirring well. Preheat oven to 350°. Spoon layer of sauce over the bottom of an 11½ x 7½-inch baking dish. Divide filling among 10 crepes; roll each crepe. Place crepes, seam side down, close together in baking dish. Spoon remaining sauce over and sprinkle with wheat germ and Parmesan cheese. Cover with foil and bake about 40 minutes or until heated through. Uncover the last 10 minutes to brown top.

OMELET

Yield: 2 servings

3 eggs
1 T. milk
   Dash of liquid red pepper sauce
¼ t. salt
1 T. butter or margarine

Beat all ingredients except butter with a whisk or rotary beater until foamy and "stringy." Heat a heavy, round-bottomed 9-inch omelet pan or skillet; when skillet is hot, a few drops of water will bounce off surface. Melt butter or margarine; coat to the top edge of the pan and quickly pour in egg mixture. "Scramble" the eggs for a moment, move omelet around to allow it to climb up the sides slightly and set. It should take only a minute to make an omelet. When it is ready, roll or fold it gently and turn out onto plate.

Note: If desired, add one or more of the following to the omelet, before cooking, during, or just before folding.

   Steamed asparagus
   Sautéed mushroom
   Sautéed zucchini
   Chopped chives and parsley
   Tender sorrel leaves
   Steamed baby Brussels sprouts
½ c. grated Colby, Cheddar, or Swiss
   cheese
   Diced green pepper
   Onion, minced
   Sautéed leeks, minced
   Steamed spinach or chard
   Any combination of minced, fresh herbs

Photograph opposite:
Jennifer's Carrot Flan

RATATOUILLE

Yield: 6 to 8 servings

2 cloves garlic, minced
1 c. thinly sliced onion
⅓ c. olive oil or a combination with vegetable oil
1 medium eggplant, peeled and diced
3 medium zucchini, sliced
2 green peppers, sliced
3 c. quartered tomatoes
1 t. oregano or ½ t. dried
1 t. sweet basil or ½ t. dried
Salt to taste
Freshly ground black pepper to taste

Sauté garlic and onion in oil over medium heat until transparent. In a large frying pan, Dutch oven, or casserole that can be used on top the stove, layer onion with the remaining ingredients, seasoning each layer with salt, pepper, and herbs. Cover and simmer 40 minutes or until vegetables are tender. If there is too much liquid, uncover and cook until it reduces. Serve hot or cold.

STUFFED CABBAGE PROVENCALE

Yield: 6 servings

1 large Savory cabbage, chilled
1 t. vegetable or olive oil
1 c. chopped onion
2 large cloves garlic, minced
1 c. fresh whole wheat bread crumbs
2 T. milk
¼ c. chopped parsley
½ c. roasted buckwheat groats (kasha)
¼ c. raw wheat germ
1 egg
¼ t. thyme
Freshly ground black pepper to taste
Salt to taste

Wash and trim cabbage; remove several outer leaves, chop, and reserve. Steam cabbage over medium heat for 15 to 20 minutes or until leaves are pliable. Remove cabbage (reserving steaming liquid); place stem side down in the center of a large piece of cheesecloth. Carefully separate leaves until core is visible. Cut out core and chop. Sauté onion, garlic, and the chopped outer leaves and core of the cabbage in oil in a large frying pan over medium heat until onion is soft. Turn off heat. Meanwhile, moisten bread crumbs with milk. Add crumbs, parsley, buckwheat groats, and wheat germ to onion mixture. Stir well and when pan is fairly cool, season to taste, and add egg. Place half of the buckwheat mixture in the center of the cabbage; distribute the rest in layers, with cabbage leaves as top layer. Reshape cabbage; brush well with olive oil. Bring cheesecloth up around cabbage and tie on top so that the cabbage holds its shape. Place cabbage in a lightly oiled deep baking dish with a tight-fitting cover (or use aluminum foil). Pour hot vegetable sauce over cabbage. Cabbage can be refrigerated at this point to be baked later or bake immediately covered in a 375° oven for 1 hour (longer if the dish has been refrigerated). Remove cover and baste cabbage; bake for 20 minutes more or until tender. Remove cheesecloth before serving, spoon Vegetable Sauce over cabbage.

VEGETABLE SAUCE OR GRAVY

1 T. vegetable oil
2 c. chopped onion
1 c. chopped carrot
2 T. whole wheat flour
2 c. liquid from steaming cabbage and/or water
¼ c. chopped parsley
½ bay leaf
Freshly ground black pepper to taste
Salt to taste

Sauté onion and carrot in oil in a large frying pan over medium heat until onion is soft. Add flour and stir until well mixed and lightly browned. Add liquid and seasonings; stir until mixture thickens. Lower heat, cover, and simmer 15 minutes more. Use when hot.

MUSHROOM AND ONION BUFFET QUICHE

Yield: 8 to 10 servings

1 lb. Swiss cheese, grated
¼ c. whole wheat flour
½ c. non-instant powdered milk
½ t. salt
  Freshly ground black pepper to taste
1 c. milk, scalded (150°)
3 eggs, beaten
3 T. margarine
1 T. vegetable oil
2 lbs. onion, minced
1 lb. mushrooms, sliced
1 t. lemon juice
2 T. dry white wine
1 unbaked whole wheat pie crust

Preheat oven to 325°. Combine grated cheese with flour, powdered milk, salt, and pepper. Let scalded milk cool; when cool, beat in eggs. Meanwhile, heat margarine and oil together in a very large skillet over medium heat until butter is melted; stir in the onion and cook until translucent. Stir in the mushrooms, lemon juice, and wine. Cover and simmer over low heat for about 8 minutes. Stir onion mixture into cheese mixture; when blended stir in egg mixture thoroughly. Place pie crust in an 11½ x 7½-inch baking dish. Pour onion-cheese mixture into the crust and bake for 40 minutes or until a table knife inserted in the center comes out clean and top is golden.

SPINACH OR CHARD QUICHE

Yield: 4 to 6 servings

1 10-oz. pkg. chopped spinach or Swiss chard
1 c. milk
½ lb. Swiss cheese, grated
2 T. whole wheat flour
¼ c. non-instant powdered milk
¼ t. salt
  Freshly ground black pepper to taste
3 eggs, beaten
1 T. minced onion
1 unbaked 10-inch pie crust

Preheat oven to 325°. Steam spinach until tender (6 to 8 minutes). Scald milk (150°) in a heavy saucepan. Combine cheese, flour, milk, salt, and pepper until the cheese is coated with flour. Stir cheese mixture into the scalded milk; add steamed spinach, and finally stir in the beaten eggs and onion. When thoroughly combined, pour mixture into pie crust and bake for 30 to 40 minutes or until a table knife inserted in the center comes out clean. This quiche can be reheated after it has been baked. Garnish with thin slices of tomato.

WHOLE WHEAT CREPES

Yield: Approximately 20

4 eggs
1 c. whole wheat pastry flour, sifted
1 c. milk
¼ c. non-instant powdered milk
1 T. vegetable oil
1 t. salt
  Butter

Beat all ingredients together with a wire whisk or rotary beater until smooth. Grease a heavy, round-bottomed crepe or omelet pan or a skillet thoroughly with butter. Place the pan over medium-high heat. When pan is hot, water drops will bounce off. Ladle batter into pan; tilt so batter covers bottom. Cook until bottom of crepe is lightly browned, turn and brown other side lightly. Place crepes on paper towels to cool until ready to use. Butter pan at regular intervals when necessary. Extras can be frozen. Crepes can be used as is, stuffed with vegetables, cheese, or a hard-boiled egg-cottage cheese-soy "beef" bits filling, rolled, and baked.

Indian and Pakistani

BLACK-EYED PEA CURRY

Yield: 6 servings

- 2 c. water or vegetable cooking liquid
- 2 10-oz. pkgs. frozen black-eyed peas
- 2 T. vegetable oil
- ½ t. cumin seeds
- 1½ c. chopped onion
- ¼ t. ground turmeric
- 1 t. ground coriander
- 1 t. ground cumin
- 1 c. Joyce's Favorite Tomato Sauce (p. 36)
  Cayenne pepper to taste
  Salt to taste
- 3 T. tamarind paste *or* 2 T. lemon juice

In a large kettle, bring water to a boil. Add the frozen peas, bring to a boil again. Cover, and simmer gently for 15 minutes. Drain, reserving ¾ cup liquid and set aside peas, covered. In a large heavy frying pan or Dutch oven, heat oil over medium heat. Toast cumin seeds in oil for a few minutes and stir in onion. Sauté onion until golden. Add turmeric, coriander, and ground cumin, heat to blend spices thoroughly. Pour in tomato sauce; let simmer for about 5 minutes, stirring occasionally. Stir in black-eyed peas, ¾ cup of cooking liquid, cayenne, salt, and the tamarind paste. Bring to a boil, cover, and simmer 25 to 35 minutes or until peas are coated with sauce. Stir often. Serve immediately.

CAULIFLOWER IN YOGURT SAUCE

Yield: 4 to 6 servings

- 1 large cauliflower
- 1 t. lemon juice
- 2 c. chopped onion
- 1 c. yogurt
- ¼ c. chopped coriander leaves
- ¼ t. ground cloves
- ½ t. ground cardamom
- 1 T. curry powder
- 1 T. chopped fresh ginger
- 2 T. vegetable oil
  Salt to taste

Freshly ground black pepper to taste
  Tomato slices
- ¼ c. chopped coriander leaves

Pour lemon juice over cauliflower; steam over medium heat for about 10 minutes. Mix together the next 7 ingredients thoroughly. Heat oil in a frying pan and stir in yogurt mixture. Simmer gently about 6 minutes; remove from heat and cool. Taste; add salt and pepper. Gently rub yogurt sauce over steamed cauliflower. Place in a saucepan with about 1 cup of steaming liquid poured into the bottom. Cover and simmer until cauliflower is tender (about 30 minutes). Baste cauliflower occasionally. Serve hot. Garnish with tomato slices and coriander leaves.

THE MEINERS' GINGERED CARROTS AND PEAS

Yield: 4 to 6 servings

- 1 2-inch piece fresh ginger, peeled
- 3 T. water
- 3 T. vegetable oil
- ¼ t. black mustard seed
- 6 fenugreek seeds
- ¼ t. turmeric
- 1 c. chopped coriander leaves, firmly packed
- 1 green or yellow chili, deseeded and chopped
- 1 lb. shelled fresh or frozen green peas
- 1½ lbs. young carrots, scrubbed and sliced
- 1 t. ground coriander
- 1 t. ground cumin
- 1 t. curry powder
- 3 T. water
- 1 t. salt

Place ginger and water in blender; blend until smooth. Heat vegetable oil in a large skillet over medium heat. Stir in mustard and fenugreek seeds; when seeds begin to pop, carefully stir in ginger mixture and turmeric. Sauté for about 2 minutes, stirring frequently. Add coriander leaves and chili. Sauté, stirring constantly, approximately 2 more minutes, adding more oil if necessary. Stir in peas and carrots; simmering for about 5 minutes, stirring frequently. Add remaining ingredients; stir thoroughly and gently. Cover, lower heat, and simmer for about 30 minutes, stirring occasionally. Serve hot.

Photograph opposite:
Black-Eyed Pea Curry

MILD EGGPLANT CURRY

Yield: 4 to 6 servings

2 c. chopped onion
3 T. vegetable oil
¾ t. chopped fresh ginger
Dash of cayenne pepper
1¼ t. ground coriander
½ t. turmeric
1 ripe tomato, chopped
2 c. tomato sauce
1 large eggplant (1½-lb.), washed and chopped
2 t. lemon juice
Salt to taste
¼ c. coriander leaves, chopped, or Italian parsley

Sauté onion in vegetable oil in a large skillet over medium heat; add ginger, cook until onions are golden. Stir in spices, tomato, and sauce; simmer until sauce is smooth. Stir in eggplant, cover thoroughly with sauce. Cover and simmer until eggplant is tender (30 to 40 minutes). Stir occasionally; if mixture becomes dry, add a little water. Stir in lemon juice. Taste and add salt; correct seasonings as desired. Serve with brown rice or pulao. Garnish with coriander leaves.

PULAO ("FANCY" RICE)

Yield: 4 to 6 servings

1 1-inch stick cinnamon
3 whole cardamoms
4 whole cloves
¼ c. slivered almonds
3 T. vegetable oil
2 c. brown rice, rinsed and picked over
5 c. water
⅓ c. yellow raisins
Salt to taste

Sauté cinnamon, cardamoms, cloves, and almonds in oil in a large skillet over medium heat until almonds are golden. Stir in rice and fry about 3 minutes. Add water and raisins and stir; bring to a boil. Reduce heat; cover and simmer on low until done (about 45 to 50 minutes). Stir in salt to taste and serve.

Italian

JOYCE'S FAVORITE TOMATO SAUCE

Yield: 4 to 5 cups sauce

1 6-oz. can tomato paste
4 to 5 c. seeded Italian plum tomatoes
1 medium green pepper, minced
1 small onion, minced
1 to 2 bay leaves
Fresh sweet basil (optional), to taste
1 t. fennel
1 t. salt
1 clove garlic, minced
1 T. olive oil

Place tomato paste and tomatoes in blender; blend until smooth. Turn mixture into a heavy-bottomed stainless steel pan; bring just to boil. Reduce heat, add remaining ingredients, and simmer, uncovered, 1 hour or until sauce is well flavored. Remove bay leaf and taste. Correct seasonings. Use immediately or freeze until needed. Recipe can easily be doubled, depending upon available tomatoes.

CAROLYN'S SICILIAN SPINACH AND RICOTTA PASTA

Yield: 4 servings

1 lb. spinach, thoroughly washed
½ lb. whole wheat egg noodles
1 c. ricotta or small curd cottage cheese
⅓ c. freshly grated Parmesan and/or Romano cheese
⅓ c. butter or margarine
Salt to taste
Freshly ground black pepper to taste

Steam spinach (or cook with just the moisture clinging to the leaves from the washing) over medium heat for 7 to 10 minutes. Drop the noodles into boiling water and stir. Cook until just tender. Mix ricotta with grated cheese. When spinach is tender, stir into ricotta mixture; add salt and pepper to taste. When noodles are tender, drain and butter thoroughly. Pour sauce over noodles, toss gently, and serve. Pass around extra grated cheese.

MARGARET'S EGGPLANT SPAGHETTI

Yield: 5 servings

⅓ c. vegetable oil
1 eggplant, cut into ½-inch cubes
⅓ c. finely chopped onion
1 clove garlic, minced
2 t. parsley flakes or 1 T. minced fresh parsley
1 28-oz. can Italian style tomatoes
1 6-oz. can tomato paste
1 10½-oz. can tomato purée
⅓ c. dry red wine
1 4-oz. can mushrooms, drained or 1 c. fresh mushrooms, braised
2 t. crushed oregano
1 t. salt
1 lb. whole wheat spaghetti, cooked until just tender and drained
Parmesan cheese freshly grated
Parsley, minced (optional)

Heat oil in Dutch oven over medium heat. Cook eggplant, onion, and garlic for 8 minutes or until onion is tender. Add remaining ingredients, up to spaghetti; stir to break up the tomatoes. Reduce heat, cover, and simmer at least 45 minutes. Pour over hot spaghetti, garnish with Parmesan cheese and parsley, if desired, and serve immediately.

LASAGNE

Yield: 6 to 8 servings

1 c. chopped onion
1 lb. mushrooms, chopped
1 lb. zucchini, chopped
2 T. butter
1 large clove garlic, minced
½ t. dried mint or 1 t. fresh, (optional)
½ t. rosemary
½ t. oregano
Salt to taste
Freshly ground black pepper to taste
4 c. Joyce's Favorite Tomato Sauce (p. 36)
1 T. vegetable oil
1 lb. whole wheat-spinach lasagne noodles
1 lb. ricotta or cottage cheese
1 lb. Mozzarella cheese, grated
1 T. minced parsley
½ c. freshly grated Romano and/or Parmesan cheese (optional)

Sauté onion, mushroom, and zucchini in butter until mushrooms begin to lose juices. Add garlic, mint, rosemary, oregano, salt, and pepper; continue cooking until vegetables are tender. Stir in tomato sauce and simmer, stirring regularly, until sauce is well-flavored and thick. Taste and correct seasonings. Boil lasagne noodles in about 6 quarts boiling water to which 1 tablespoon vegetable oil has been added. Cook until just tender (5 to 7 minutes); drain. Separate slices so they won't stick together during assembling. Preheat oven to 350°. Mix together Mozzarella and ricotta cheese with parsley. Lightly grease an 8 x 12 x 2-inch baking dish. Spoon tomato sauce on the bottom. Layer with lasagne noodles, ricotta mixture and sauce, ending with the tomato sauce. Sprinkle on Parmesan cheese, if desired. Bake, uncovered, 30 minutes or until heated through. Let stand 5 minutes before cutting into squares. Can be made ahead and baked at serving time, or served cold the second day.

PESTO OVER WHOLE WHEAT OR SPINACH NOODLES

Yield: 4 to 6 servings

1 c. minced fresh basil or 1/3 c. dried
½ c. minced parsley
1 large clove garlic
½ c. freshly grated Romano and/or Parmesan cheese
¼ c. almonds or walnuts
¼ t. salt
Freshly ground black pepper to taste
¼ c. olive oil
1 lb. whole wheat or spinach noodles
¼ c. butter

Place basil, parsley, garlic, cheese, almonds, salt, and pepper in blender; blend until smooth. Add olive oil gradually (in a thin, steady stream) until mixture is the consistency of soft butter. You can refrigerate at this point until needed. Cook noodles until just tender; drain and toss in butter. Add approximately ¾ of the almond mixture (Pesto) and toss again. Serve immediately. Pass remaining Pesto and additional Romano and/or Parmesan cheese.

TOFU-NOODLE BAKE

Yield: 4 to 6 servings

1 T. vegetable oil
¾ c. minced onion
2 cloves garlic, minced
1 rib celery, minced
¼ c. minced green pepper
1 c. tofu, drained and patted dry
½ c. cottage cheese, drained
1 egg, slightly beaten
1 T. whole wheat flour
1 T. minced parsley
1 t. oregano
1 T. minced chives
   Salt to taste
   Freshly ground black pepper to taste
½ lb. whole wheat noodles
1 c. Joyce's Favorite Tomato Sauce with
   sweet basil, (p. 36)
¼ c. raw wheat germ
¼ c. freshly grated Parmesan cheese

In a medium-sized skillet, sauté onion, garlic, celery, and green pepper until onion is translucent. Mash tofu and mix in cottage cheese, egg, flour, parsley, oregano, and chives. Combine tofu mixture with onion mixture; add salt and pepper to taste. Cook noodles in boiling water until just tender; drain. Preheat oven to 350°. Grease a 2-quart casserole; spread half the cooked noodles evenly over the bottom of the casserole. Cover with tofu/onion mixture. Spread remaining noodles on top. Pour tomato sauce over noodles, and sprinkle wheat germ and Parmesan cheese over all. Bake for about 40 minutes or until heated through and bubbly.

CAROLYN'S SPAGHETTI

Yield: 6 servings

1½ lb. whole wheat spaghetti
   Salt
2 T. olive oil
1 c. chopped onion
1½ lb. ripe tomatoes, chopped
½ t. marjoram
   Freshly ground black pepper to taste
½ c. soy "bacon" bits
1 c. freshly grated Parmesan and/or
   Romano cheese

Bring a large pan of water to a boil; add spaghetti, salt to taste and let boil until just tender (about 8 to 10 minutes). Sauté onion in olive oil until transparent. Stir in tomatoes, marjoram, and pepper. Simmer briskly, stirring regularly, for about 10 minutes until spaghetti is tender. Drain spaghetti. Add "bacon" bits to tomato sauce; taste, and correct seasonings. Pour sacue over spaghetti, sprinkle on grated cheese, and serve immediately.

Middle Eastern

SPANAKOPITTA
(SPINACH PIE)

Yield: 24 servings

2 lbs. (or 2 10-oz. boxes) fresh spinach or
   Swiss chard, chopped
½ c. butter or margarine, melted
10 sheets filo pastry
½ lb. feta cheese or Gruyere or Cheddar
1 c. small curd cottage cheese
3 eggs, well beaten
   Freshly ground black pepper to taste
   Freshly grated nutmeg
   Salt to taste

Steam spinach until just tender (5 to 8 minutes). Preheat oven to 375°. Butter an 11 x 17-inch jelly roll or similar baking pan. Brush butter on each of 5 filo sheets, place on bottom of pan. (Keep remaining filo sheets thoroughly covered with a damp cloth.) Drain spinach and stir in feta cheese, cottage cheese, eggs, pepper, nutmeg, and salt. Place the spinach mixture on the filo sheets in baking dish; make certain to spread filling almost to the edges of the pastry. Place remaining filo sheets on top, brushing butter on each sheet as you assemble. (You can bake this dish later; it keeps well in the refrigerator wrapped in foil.) Cover baking sheet with foil and bake for about thirty minutes. Remove foil and continue baking until Spanakopitta is golden. Cut into squares or diamonds and serve immediately.

Photograph opposite:
Spanakopitta

SANDRA'S DOLMAS (STUFFED GRAPE LEAVES)

Yield: Approximately 25 dolmas

¼ lb. grapevine leaves (approximately 25) either from a jar, in brine, or picked fresh, unwashed, and frozen
6 to 8 cloves garlic
Juice of ½ lemon
1 T. minced mint (optional)
Filling

Rinse preserved vine leaves thoroughly to drain off most of the salt; if leaves are not pliable, pour boiling water over; let soak 15 to 20 minutes. Drain again; pour cold water over them. If still too salty, repeat process. A similar method works for fresh-frozen grapevine leaves. Wash thoroughly; pour boiling water over several times until limp. Remove stems. Choose a filling; divide filling among the leaves and place on rib side, near stem edge. Turn stem edge and sides in toward rib and over filling, roll tightly so no filling can cook out. When ready to cook, place leftover or broken vine leaves on the bottom of a heavy saucepan, pour in a small amount of water, pack dolmas tightly in layers, alternating the directions of the layers, and sprinkle each layer with lemon juice. Push garlic cloves among dolmas; add mint, if desired. Place a plate upside down on top of dolmas, and simmer, covered, 1½ to 2 hours or until tender. Serve hot. Leftovers can be served cold.

FILLING #1

1 c. cooked brown rice
½ c. minced green onion
3 T. minced parsley
½ t. allspice
¼ c. currants
¼ c. chopped walnuts
2 cloves garlic, minced
Freshly ground black pepper to taste
Salt to taste

FILLING #2

1 c. cooked brown rice
½ c. minced green onion
2 T. minced fresh mint
½ t. cinnamon
2 T. minced parsley
½ t. allspice
2 cloves garlic, minced
Freshly ground black pepper to taste
Salt to taste

FILLING #3

1 c. cooked brown rice
½ c. soy "beef" bits
3 T. minced fresh mint
½ c. minced onion
4 T. minced parsley
½ t. allspice
Salt to taste
Freshly ground black pepper to taste

FILLING #4

¾ c. cooked brown rice
½ c. ground or chopped cooked chick-peas
3 T. minced parsley
½ t. allspice
1 clove garlic, minced
1 T. minced fresh mint leaves
½ c. minced onion
Salt to taste
Freshly ground black pepper to taste

Mix together the ingredients of whichever filling you choose. Taste and correct seasonings. Fill vine leaves.

Note: For a crowd, make all four fillings. Fill one pound of vine leaves with the fillings, and simmer them all in a large, heavy pan.

MARY'S KASHA

Yield: 4 servings

1 egg, slightly beaten
1 c. kasha (buckwheat groats)
2 c. boiling Vegetable Broth (p. 15) or other vegetable cooking liquid.
Salt to taste
Freshly ground black pepper to taste

Mix egg and kasha together. Pour into a hot iron frying pan, stirring until kernels separate. When mixture is dry, pour into boiling liquid. Cover, reduce heat and let simmer 20 minutes or until tender. Add salt and pepper to taste. Serve with braised mushrooms, sautéed onions, toasted almonds, or vegetable gravy.

Mexican

LYNN'S QUICK CORN AND CHILI CASSEROLE

Yield: 4 to 6 servings

- 2 1-lb. cans cream-style corn
- 4 eggs, beaten
- ¾ c. cornmeal
- 2 cloves garlic, minced
- 4 T. vegetable oil
- 2 to 3 yellow chilies or 2 or more green chilies to taste, minced
- 2 c. grated sharp Cheddar cheese

Preheat oven to 350°. Mix together corn, eggs, cornmeal, garlic, and vegetable oil. Place half of the corn mixture into a greased 2-quart casserole. Sprinkle on chilies and cheese; pour remaining half of corn mixture on top. Bake 45 minutes or until mixture is firm and lightly golden. Serve immediately.

ENCHILADAS

Yield: 8 servings

FILLING

- 1 T. vegetable or olive oil
- 1 large clove garlic, minced
- ½ c. chopped green onion
- 3 T. chopped pimiento-stuffed olives
- 2 t. chili powder
- 1 c. cooked red beans, undrained
- ½ c. soy "beef" bits
  Salt to taste
  Freshly ground black pepper to taste
- 8 stone-ground tortillas
  Vegetable oil
- 1½ c. grated sharp Cheddar cheese
  Ripe olives, sliced

Sauté garlic and onion in oil until onion is tender. Stir in olives, chili powder, and beans. When mixture is thoroughly blended and hot, remove from heat; add soy bits, and season to taste. Set aside. Make Sauce. Fry tortillas in oil until lightly browned but still pliable. Drain on paper towels. While still hot fill each with ⅛ of the bean filling. Roll up carefully. Preheat oven to 350°. Pour ¾ of the tomato sauce into the bottom of an 11½ x 7½-inch baking dish. Place tortillas on top, seam side down, and cover with re-maining Sauce. Sprinkle with cheese and olives. Bake about 25 minutes or until heated through.

SAUCE

- 1 T. vegetable or olive oil
- 1 c. chopped onion
- ½ green pepper, chopped
- 2 large cloves garlic, chopped
- 1 yellow or green chili pepper, chopped
- 4 c. canned tomatoes and juice
- 1 6-oz. can tomato paste
- 1 T. chili powder
  Salt to taste

Sauté onion, green pepper, garlic, and chili pepper together in oil until onion is tender. Add tomatoes, tomato paste, and chili powder. Let simmer, uncovered, about ½ hour. Season to taste.

BULGUR WHEAT CHILI

Yield: 4 to 6 servings

- 1 T. vegetable oil
- ½ c. onion
- ⅔ c. bulgur wheat
- 1⅓ c. water or vegetable cooking liquid
- 1 c. tomato sauce
- 2 c. cooked kidney, red, or pinto beans
- 1 T. chili powder
- ½ t. oregano
- ½ t. sweet basil
  Freshly ground black pepper to taste
  Salt to taste
  Sharp Cheddar cheese, grated (optional)

In a large frying pan, sauté onion in vegetable oil. Stir in bulgur and let toast slightly. Add water; cover, and let simmer 10 to 15 minutes or until bulgur becomes tender. Add remaining ingredients; salt and pepper to taste. Heat to serving temperature. (Chili tastes better if it can be refrigerated for several hours or overnight, allowing seasonings to blend.) Garnish with cheese, if desired.

Note: If you prefer more beans than cracked wheat in your chili, reduce the amount of wheat and cooking liquid or double the beans and tomato sauce. Correct seasonings.

Oriental

SUKIYAKI

Yield: 4 to 6 servings

2 c. green onion, cut into 3-inch lengths
1 c. celery, diagonally cut into 2-inch slices
½ lb. mushrooms, washed and thinly sliced
1 5-oz. can water chestnuts, drained and thinly sliced
1 5-oz. can bamboo shoots, drained and slivered
1 lb. fresh mung bean sprouts
5 c. spinach or chard leaves, chopped into medium-sized pieces
½ lb. tofu, cut into 1-inch cubes
2 T. honey
½ c. soy sauce
½ c. Vegetable Broth (p. 15)
1 to 2 T. vegetable oil

Arrange vegetables attractively on a large platter or tray. Mix honey, soy sauce and broth together in a small pitcher. At the table in an electric wok or skillet, heat vegetable oil over medium heat. Stir in onion with chopsticks or large spoon and fork and stir-fry 1 minute. Stir in about ¼ cup sauce (electric skillet will require more than wok) and let heat. Push onion aside. Add remaining vegetables, in order given, stir-frying for 1 minute and pushing aside. When all ingredients have been heated through, serve with brown rice. Pass soy sauce.

Photograph opposite:
Sukiyaki

TEMPURA UNLIMITED

Yield: 4 to 6 servings

Vegetables for frying
1 c. whole wheat flour, sifted
2 T. rice flour
½ t. salt
1 egg, beaten thoroughly
1¼ c. ice water
4 c. vegetable oil plus sesame oil (approximately)

Select well-chilled vegetables, such as carrot, onion, cauliflower, parsnips, broccoli, and green pepper. Thoroughly scrub vegetables and cut into long sticks, flowerets, or rings. Mix flours and salt together in a medium-sized bowl. Pour in egg and water gradually, beating continuously. When mixture is smooth, refrigerate. Dust vegetables with whole wheat flour, if slippery, then dip into batter. To fry, pour 3 inches of vegetable oil into deep fryer. Add sesame oil to taste. Heat to 350°. Place a few batter-dipped vegetables into the hot oil. Deep-fry for 5 to 10 minutes or until batter is golden. Drain on paper towels and serve immediately with soy sauce and brown rice.

FRIED RICE

Yield: 4 servings

2 to 3 T. vegetable oil
½ c. chopped green onion
½ c. chopped carrot
½ c. chopped celery
½ c. chopped green pepper
1 c. fresh or frozen small green peas
¼ c. soy sauce
4 to 5 c. leftover cooked brown rice
1 egg, slightly beaten
1 c. fresh bean sprouts
¼ c. soy "bacon" bits

Heat oil in wok or electric frying pan; stir-fry onion, carrot, celery, and green pepper until vegetables are tender-crisp. Stir in peas and soy sauce and add brown rice; cook until thoroughly hot. Move rice and vegetables to one side, pour in egg (add a little oil where egg will be poured), and stir-fry until scrambled. Add bean sprouts, stir mixture together and heat through. Sprinkle on "bacon" bits and serve immediately.

Vegetable Side Dishes

MOM'S SWEET 'N SOUR YELLOW BEANS

Yield: 4 to 6 servings

1 lb. yellow beans (approximately 4 cups), fresh or frozen
2 T. brown sugar, well-packed
2 t. cornstarch
¼ c. cider vinegar
  Salt to taste
  Freshly ground black pepper to taste

Slice yellow beans as desired. Steam until tender (about 10 minutes). In a heavy-bottomed saucepan, mix together brown sugar and cornstarch. Add vinegar. Simmer over medium heat, stirring constantly. When sauce is thickened and clear, pour over hot beans. Add salt and pepper to taste; toss gently until all beans are coated with sauce. Serve hot or cold.

STIR-FRIED CABBAGE OR BRUSSELS SPROUTS

Yield: 4 servings

2 T. vegetable oil
1 c. chopped onion
1 large clove garlic, minced
1 lb. cabbage or Brussels sprouts, chilled and chopped
1 T. soy sauce (or to taste)
  Salt
  Freshly ground black pepper
3 T. water
1 T. cornstarch

Heat oil in a large frying pan; sauté onion and garlic until transparent. Add cabbage or sprouts, increase heat, and stir constantly for 3 or 4 minutes. Add soy sauce, salt, and pepper to taste. Continue to cook and stir constantly another 3 to 4 minutes. Combine water and cornstarch until smooth. Pour into cabbage mixture and stir until cornstarch mixture is clear. Serve immediately while piping hot.

MOM'S DILLED GREEN BEANS

Yield: 4 servings

1 T. vegetable oil
2 to 3 T. water
2 c. sliced fresh or frozen green beans
½ c. bean sprouts
¼ c. chopped green onion
1 T. chopped pimiento (optional)
1 T. cider vinegar
½ t. dill weed
  Freshly ground black pepper to taste
  Salt to taste

Heat oil in wok or electric skillet; add water (less for wok) and green beans. Cook until tender (approximately 6 to 7 minutes). Add remaining ingredients, toss lightly and heat through. Serve immediately.

MARY'S CAULIFLOWER IN CHEESE SAUCE

Yield: 4 to 6 servings

2 c. milk
¼ t. salt
2 T. butter or margarine
3 T. whole wheat flour
1 c. grated Herkimer or strong, white Canadian Cheddar cheese
1 T. lemon juice
1 large whole cauliflower

In a heavy bottomed sauce pan, mix together milk and salt. Heat almost to a boil. Meanwhile, melt butter in a heavy skillet, stir in flour, sauté for about 2 minutes, stirring constantly. Do not allow mixture to scorch. Add hot milk all at once; stir with a wire whisk until sauce comes to a boil. Boil for about 1 minute, stirring constantly. Remove from heat, taste, and correct seasonings. Stir in cheese. Pour lemon juice over cauliflower and steam until tender (20 to 25 minutes). Pour cheese sauce over hot cauliflower and serve immediately.

ONE SKILLET EGGPLANT DINNER

Yield: 4 servings

1 medium eggplant, sliced into ¼-inch circles
  Vegetable oil
1 medium green pepper, sliced
1 small onion, minced
1 clove garlic, minced
2 c. tomato sauce
  Oregano
  Sweet basil
  Freshly ground black pepper
1 c. grated Cheddar or colby cheese
¼ c. freshly grated Parmesan cheese

Pour enough vegetable oil into a large frying pan to coat. Fry eggplant gently until browned on both sides. Add more oil as necessary. Turn down heat, add vegetables, pour tomato sauce over all. If tomato sauce does not contain herbs, add oregano and sweet basil to taste. Add black pepper if needed. Sprinkle cheeses on top. Cover tightly and let simmer until eggplant is tender (30 minutes or less.) Serve with pasta or as desired.

AUNT RUTH'S ONION CASSEROLE

Yield: 4 to 6 servings

1 lb. small onions, peeled
1 c. water
¾ c. tomato juice mixed with ¼ c. steaming liquid
1 T. cornstarch
½ c. whole wheat bread crumbs
  Butter or margarine
  Freshly ground black pepper to taste

In a saucepan steam onions in 1 cup water until barely tender, 8 to 10 minutes. Mix tomato juice and cornstarch together; heat in a casserole dish that can be used on top of the stove. When tomato juice mixture has thickened, stir in onions until all are coated. (If tomato sauce seems too thick, dilute with a little more water.) Sprinkle bread crumbs on top, dot with butter; season with pepper. Can be made ahead and baked later at this point. When ready to bake, preheat oven to 350°. Cover and bake about 40 minutes or until onions are tender and heated through. To brown the crumbs, remove the cover the final minutes of baking.

PARSNIP-STUFFED ZUCCHINI

Yield: 6 servings

3 medium-size zucchini, sliced lengthwise
3 medium-size parsnips, cubed
2 T. chopped onion
  Butter or margarine
  Salt to taste
  Freshly ground black pepper to taste

In a small amount of water, steam zucchini and parsnips until tender (6 to 8 minutes). Mash parsnips with onion; add butter, salt, and pepper to taste. Scoop centers out of the zucchini; add to parsnip mixture. Correct seasonings. Fill zucchini with parsnip stuffing. Can be made ahead and baked at serving time. Preheat oven to 400°. Place the zucchini in a well-greased baking dish, cover and bake 15 to 20 minutes or until thoroughly heated and tender.

HOLLANDAISE SAUCE FOR VEGETABLES

Yield: About 1 cup

½ c. margarine or butter
3 egg yolks at room temperature
1½ T. lemon juice
¼ t. dry mustard
¼ t. salt
  Freshly ground black pepper

In a small saucepan, melt butter until bubbly. Place egg yolks, lemon juice, mustard, and seasonings into blender container; cover and blend on low until yolks are frothy. Pour in half the butter in a very slow, steady stream until creamy. Then turn blender to high and add remaining butter slowly. Taste and correct seasonings. Serve immediately on steamed vegetables such as Brussels sprouts, broccoli, zucchini. If reheated, warm the sauce gently over hot water, stirring carefully.

BROCCOLI CASSEROLE

Yield: 8 servings

3 to 4 c. chopped broccoli
⅓ c. finely chopped onion
4 T. margarine
3 T. whole wheat pastry flour
½ c. vegetable cooking water or broth
¾ c. grated Cheddar cheese
3 eggs, well-beaten
½ c. whole wheat bread crumbs
1 T. butter or margarine

Preheat oven to 325°. Melt 4 tablespoons margarine in a large skillet over medium heat; stir in onion and broccoli; sauté covered, until broccoli is barely tender. (If using frozen broccoli, drop about 20 ounces into a small amount of boiling water, cover, and cook quickly. Add to skillet and use the cooking water later in the recipe.) Stir flour into the onion-broccoli mixture and let cook a minute or so. Add cooking water or broth; stir until thickened. Lower heat and quickly stir in cheese until well blended. Remove from heat and gradually stir in eggs. Pour into a well greased 1½ to 2-quart casserole. Pour crumbs over and dot with butter. Bake for 30 minutes or until done.

DELUXE GREEN BEANS

Yield: 6 servings

3 c. sliced fresh or frozen green beans
2 T. margarine or butter
⅓ c. chopped onion
2 T. whole wheat flour
½ t. salt
Freshly ground black pepper to taste
1 c. dairy sour cream
½ c. grated Cheddar cheese

Steam beans until tender (about 10 minutes). Preheat oven to 350°. Melt butter in a small, heavy-bottomed pan; add onion and sauté until tender. Stir in flour, salt, and pepper. When thoroughly mixed, add the sour cream very carefully and heat. Do not boil. Taste and correct seasonings. Stir sour cream mixture into hot beans; pour beans into a greased 1-quart casserole. Top with cheese. Bake about 15 minutes or until cheese melts and beans are heated thoroughly. Serve.

Photograph opposite:
Deluxe Green Beans

ZUCCHINI AND CHEESE CASSEROLE

Yield: 6 servings

2 lbs. zucchini (about 6 medium)
½ lb. sharp Cheddar cheese
Salt to taste
Freshly ground black pepper to taste

Preheat oven to 350°. Scrub and grate zucchini; grate cheese. Grease a 2-quart casserole dish. Place a layer of zucchini on the bottom and cover it with a layer of cheese. Salt and pepper to taste. Keep on layering until you have six layers, the cheese on top; continue to salt and pepper to taste. Bake, covered, for approximately 40 minutes or until done.

BERNICE ROTH'S RED CABBAGE

Yield: 6 to 8 servings

1 head red cabbage, chopped
¾ c. chopped onion
1 T. vegetable oil
⅛ t. allspice
1 raw apple, chopped
¼ c. dry white wine or vermouth
1 T. brown sugar
Salt to taste
Freshly ground black pepper to taste

In a large frying pan, stir-fry cabbage and onion in vegetable oil until cabbage is just tender. Add allspice and raw apple and continue to stir until apple is hot. Add wine and brown sugar; taste and season as desired. When thoroughly heated, serve.

JOYCE'S FRIED CAULIFLOWER

Yield: 6 servings

1 head cauliflower, broken into flowerets (or can use zucchini or artichoke hearts)
1 egg, well-beaten
½ t. salt
¼ c. unbleached flour
¼ c. water

Pour 1 inch of olive oil into a small, deep iron pan. Stir remaining ingredients except cauliflower together; coat the flowerets in the batter. Fry cauliflowerets a few at a time, for a few minutes in hot oil; drain thoroughly on paper towels. Keep cooked vegetables on a warm platter in oven until serving time. (This dish can be made ahead. Reheat before serving for about 10 minutes in a 400° oven.)

Salads

ROASTED PEPPER SALAD

Yield: 6 servings

6 large green peppers (or 3 red and 3 green)
¼ c. olive or vegetable oil
1 T. wine vinegar
1 large clove garlic, minced
⅛ t. salt
Freshly ground black pepper to taste
Parsley, minced

Place peppers under broiler; turn regularly until they are blistered thoroughly. Wrap peppers in a damp towel and set aside until cool. Peel and cut peppers into quarters or sixths, discard seeds and membranes. Mix oil, vinegar, garlic, salt, and pepper together in a medium-sized mixing bowl; add peppers and let marinate, covered, in the refrigerator for at least 3 to 4 hours. Occasionally, stir gently. When ready to serve, drain, arrange on a serving dish, and garnish with parsley, if desired.

ROGER'S RAITA
(INDIAN CUCUMBER, TOMATO, AND YOGURT SALAD)

Yield: 6 servings

2 c. plain yogurt
1 large cucumber, chopped
2 ripe tomatoes, chopped
6 to 8 scallions, chopped
Freshly ground black pepper to taste
½ t. cumin seed
Salt to taste
Dash of cayenne pepper (optional)
Paprika

Beat yogurt until smooth. Toast cumin seed for 2 to 3 minutes in a heavy frying pan and crush. Stir cucumber, tomatoes, scallions, black pepper, and a pinch of cumin into yogurt; add salt to taste. Add cayenne if desired. Garnish with paprika and another pinch of cumin. Chill until ready to serve.

SUNCHOKE SALAD

Yield: 4 to 6 servings

1 lb. sunchokes (Jerusalem artichokes)
2 t. lemon juice
½ c. minced onion
2 T. minced green pepper
2 ribs celery, minced
1 carrot, grated
½ c. mayonnaise
1 t. prepared mustard
Freshly ground black pepper to taste
Salt to taste
Garnishes: Paprika; hard-boiled egg slices; minced parsley

Scrub chokes and steam until tender (about 12 minutes.) Chill. Peel chokes and slice into a medium-sized serving dish. Sprinkle with lemon; add remaining ingredients except pepper, and salt, and the garnishes. Toss gently; add salt and pepper to taste. Garnish and serve cold.

LIMA BEAN SALAD

Yield: 4 to 6 servings

1½ c. dried lima beans
3 c. water
⅔ c. chopped green onion
2 hard-boiled eggs, chopped
Freshly ground black pepper to taste
Salt to taste
Parsley, chopped
½ c. pitted black olives

Soak beans in water overnight; the next day simmer 2 to 2½ hours or until beans are tender. Add more water if needed. Drain, and cool the beans. Mix with remaining ingredients; pour your favorite vinegar and oil dressing over; chill until served.

QUICK WINTER SALAD

Yield: 10 to 12 servings

1 1-lb. can garbanzo beans, drained
1 small bunch radishes, sliced
1 T. olive oil
1 1-lb. can kidney beans, drained
3 ribs celery, chopped
1 T. wine vinegar
1 1-lb. can lima beans, drained
1 green pepper, chopped
2 to 4 mushrooms, sliced
2 T. lemon juice
½ t. paprika
  Salt to taste
  Freshly ground black pepper to taste
  Salad greens
  Parsley, chopped

Mix garbanzos, radishes, and olive oil together. In separate bowl, mix kidney beans, celery, and wine vinegar. In third bowl mix together lima beans, green pepper, mushrooms, and lemon juice. Sprinkle paprika on top. Chill bowls for about 1 hour. Taste each; add salt and pepper to taste. Drizzle a small amount of olive oil on the lima beans; put a small amount of vinegar or lemon juice on the garbanzos. Put each bean mixture into a separate section on a large serving tray. Garnish with salad greens and dust with parsley.

GARDEN MACARONI SALAD

Yield: 6 to 8 servings

2 c. cooked whole wheat macaroni, chilled
½ c. chopped tart apples
½ c. mayonnaise
1 c. freshly shelled large green peas
½ c. diced celery
2 hard-boiled eggs
1 green pepper
  Freshly ground black pepper to taste
  Salt to taste
  Crisp lettuce (optional)

In a large serving bowl, mix together macaroni, apples, mayonnaise, peas, and celery. Dice one egg and half of the green pepper; stir into salad. Taste and add salt and pepper as desired. Slice the other egg; garnish salad with egg slices and diced green pepper. Serve on lettuce leaves, if desired.

CLASSIC GREEN SALAD

Yield: 8 servings

8 c. fresh, washed, crisp young greens*
1 clove garlic, split
⅓ c. sliced radishes
  Parsley
  Chives

Tear greens into bite-size pieces. Rub garlic clove against the inside of a salad bowl. Add greens to bowl. Garnish with radishes, parsley, and chives. Pour about half of the dressing over salad; toss well and serve.

*Note: Choose from spinach, chard, various lettuces, curly endive, watercress, mustard and turnip greens, and collards.

GARLIC DRESSING

Yield: 1 cup

¾ c. olive and/or vegetable oil
¼ c. wine vinegar
½ t. salt
  Freshly ground black pepper to taste
1 clove garlic, minced (optional)

Mix all ingredients together thoroughly. Taste and correct seasoning.

CUCUMBERS IN SOUR CREAM

Yield: 6 servings

2 large cucumbers, peeled, and sliced
2 T. sour cream
1½ T. mayonnaise
3 T. chopped fresh dill or 2 T. dill seed
  Freshly ground black pepper to taste

Mix all ingredients together in a serving dish; refrigerate for at least 1 hour before serving. Taste and correct seasonings.

CHEF'S SALAD

Yield: 6 large servings

1 clove garlic
½ c. olive oil or a vegetable-olive
   oil combination
1 c. whole wheat bread cubes
2 heads crisp Romaine, washed and dried
4 green onions, chopped
¾ c. slivered Swiss or other cheese
3 ripe tomatoes, quartered
½ t. dry mustard
   Dash of Worcestershire sauce
2 T. wine vinegar
   Freshly ground black pepper to taste
1 t. salt
1 coddled egg
   Juice of 1 lemon
¼ c. freshly grated Parmesan cheese

Mash garlic clove into oil and let flavors blend as long as possible, preferably overnight. Sauté bread cubes in 2 tablespoons of the garlic oil, drain; set aside and cool on paper towels. Coddle egg 1½ minutes in simmering water. Tear lettuce into bite-sized pieces; place in a large salad bowl. Add onion, cheese, and tomatoes. Pour the remaining garlic oil on salad; toss lightly until coated well. Add dry mustard, Worcestershire sauce, and wine vinegar; toss again. Season with pepper and salt; break coddled egg onto salad. Squeeze lemon onto egg; sprinkle with Parmesan cheese. Toss again and garnish with bread cubes.

MOM'S CARROT AND RAISIN SALAD

Yield: 6 to 8 servings

3 c. grated raw carrots
1 c. seedless raisins
1 T. honey
6 T. mayonnaise
¼ c. milk
1 T. fresh lemon juice
¼ t. salt

Toss carrots and raisins together. Blend remaining ingredients and pour over carrots and raisins. Stir carefully and thoroughly. Chill to blend flavors.

GREEK SALAD

Yield: 6 servings

⅓ c. olive oil or vegetable oil
   Juice of one lemon
2 T. chopped fresh oregano *or* 1 T. dried
4 T. minced parsley
   Freshly ground black pepper to taste
   Salt (optional)
1 head crisp lettuce, torn into bite-sized
   pieces
1 green pepper, seeds and membrane
   removed and sliced lengthwise
2 to 3 tomatoes, cut into sixths
½ c. crumbled feta cheese
12 black olives
1 red onion, sliced into rings
1 hard-boiled egg, sliced

Combine oil, lemon juice, and seasonings. Taste and correct seasonings. Pour into a cruet. Remove seeds and membranes from green pepper; slice lengthwise. On individual serving plates, place lettuce, pepper, and tomatoes. Divide cheese, olives, and onion slices among the plates. Garnish with egg. Pour a small amount of the oil and lemon juice mixture on each salad, pass the rest.

CUB SCOUT'S FRUIT SALAD

Yield: 12 servings

2 pears, cored and chopped
1 bunch grapes, seeds removed
2 oranges, peeled and chopped
2 apples, cored and chopped
2 c. canned pineapple chunks
¾ c. raisins (optional)
¾ c. shredded coconut
2 bananas, chopped
   Lemon juice
¼ c. tofu
¼ c. plain yogurt
1 c. cherry yogurt

Sprinkle apples and banana with lemon juice. In a very large serving bowl, mix all the fruits together. Mix together the tofu and yogurt in a blender until smooth. Stir together with cherry yogurt; pour over fruit. Toss gently. Serve cold.

Photograph opposite:
Greek Salad

MOM'S BULGUR SALAD

Yield: 4 to 6 servings

- 1 c. bulgur wheat (cracked wheat)
- 2 c. boiling water
  Salt to taste
- ½ c. chopped green onion
- ½ c. diced or grated carrot
- ½ c. diced celery
- 2 tomatoes, sliced into sixths
- ½ c. alfalfa sprouts
- ⅔ c. minced parsley
  Freshly ground black pepper to taste

Pour boiling water over wheat in a small bowl; cover and let stand about 30 minutes. Drain. Place fluffed bulgur into a large serving bowl. Let cool completely. Salt lightly to taste. Add remaining ingredients. Pour dressing over the salad and correct seasonings. Serve cold; may be garnished with lettuce leaves.

DRESSING

- 6 T. olive oil
- 2 t. wine vinegar
  Salt to taste

Mix all ingredients together well.

STUFFED TOMATO LUNCHEON SALAD

Yield: 6 servings

- 6 ripe tomatoes
- 6 ribs celery, minced
- 1 green pepper, minced
- 1 c. peanuts or chopped walnuts
- ⅓ c. plain yogurt
  Salt (optional)
  Freshly ground black pepper to taste
  Paprika
  Shredded lettuce

Slice six gashes into each tomato approximately halfway down. Scoop out as much tomato as desired. Mix together celery, green pepper, nuts, and yogurt. Taste; add salt and pepper. Divide stuffing among tomato cases; sprinkle with paprika. Chill until serving time. Serve on top of shredded lettuce.

LENTIL SALAD

Yield: 12 servings

- 5 c. water, vegetable cooking liquid, or broth
- 1 lb. dried lentils
- 1 c. chopped red onion
- 4 garlic cloves, peeled and chopped
- 1 rib celery, chopped
- 1 carrot, chopped
- 1 t. thyme
- 1 t. sweet basil
- 1 t. oregano
- ½ c. chopped parsley
- 5 green onions, minced
- 1 green pepper, chopped

Bring water to a boil in a large kettle; add remaining ingredients, except green onion and green pepper. Turn heat down, cover, and simmer 1½ hours or until lentils are tender. You may need to add a little water as lentils cook. Pour dressing over cooked lentils. Let cool and refrigerate. Add salt and pepper as desired and garnish with onions and green pepper before serving.

VINEGAR AND OIL DRESSING

- ½ c. vegetable oil
- 3 T. wine vinegar
- 1 T. prepared mustard
  Freshly ground black pepper to taste
  Salt to taste

Combine ingredients, mixing well.

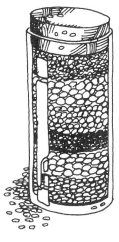

Desserts

SESAME SEED COOKIES

Yield: 3 dozen cookies

1¾ c. whole wheat flour
¼ c. soy flour
1 t. baking powder
¼ t. salt
½ c. margarine
¾ c. brown sugar, firmly packed
1 egg
2 T. toasted sesame seeds
1 T. water
2 T. raw sesame seeds

Mix flours, baking powder and salt together. Cream sugar with margarine; beat in egg and stir in toasted sesame seeds. Add flour mixture alternately with water. Chill dough 3 to 4 hours. Drop dough by teaspoonfuls onto greased cookie sheets. Flatten with a glass dipped in flour. Sprinkle extra raw sesame seeds on top. Bake in a preheated 375° oven for 10 minutes or until lightly browned around edges.

PUMPKIN PIE

Yield: 10-inch pie

2 c. pumpkin purée
⅔ c. brown sugar
½ t. salt
1 t. cinnamon
¾ t. ginger
½ t. nutmeg
⅛ t. cloves
3 eggs, beaten
1 6-oz. can evaporated milk
1¼ c. milk
1 t. nutritional yeast
1 10-inch unbaked pastry shell

Preheat oven to 400°. Combine pumpkin, sugar, salt and spices. Add eggs, milk, and nutritional yeast; mix well. Pour into pastry shell. Bake about 50 minutes or until knife inserted in center comes out clean.

GRAHAM-MILK CRACKERS

Yield: 5 dozen medium crackers

4 c. whole wheat pastry flour or graham flour
¾ c. butter or margarine, chilled
⅔ c. brown sugar, firmly packed
1 t. cinnamon
2 T. nutritional yeast
1½ t. salt
1 t. baking powder
1 c. milk, cold

With a pastry blender or fork, blend flour and butter together until mixture resembles crumbs. Add rest of dry ingredients and mix well. Add milk slowly until mixture forms a smooth ball. Preheat oven to 400°. Knead dough until smooth, 5 to 10 minutes. Roll out ⅛-inch thick on a floured cloth with a floured rolling pin. Cut into desired shapes with cookie cutters (or into squares, diamonds, or rectangles). Place on well-greased baking sheets, prick a design with a fork, if desired, and bake 6 to 8 minutes or until lightly browned. Remove from sheets and let cool on wire racks. Store in tightly covered tin.

CRUNCHY PEANUT BUTTER TREATS

Yield: 2 dozen balls or 6 "cups"

¾ c. crunchy granola
½ c. non-instant powdered milk
½ c. non-hydrogenated chunky peanut butter
¼ c. honey

In a small bowl; mix together the ingredients until thoroughly combined. Form into balls or spread in 2½-inch paper liners placed in muffin tins. Chill.

RHUBARB (OR APPLE) CRUMBLE

Yield: 8 servings

4 c. chopped rhubarb (or tart apples,
cored, but unpeeled, or a combination
of both)

1 t. lemon juice (if more tartness or flavor
is desired)

½ c. honey (more or less, depending upon
tartness of fruit)

Preheat oven to 350°. Place rhubarb in a
9-inch, 1¼-inch deep pie plate. Pour honey
over all. Pour Topping on fruit. Bake for 30
minutes or until fruit is tender when tested
with a fork.

Note: You can have fun experimenting with
this easy-to-make crumble. For example,
mix raisins with the fruit, mix raw sunflower
or sesame seeds or chopped nuts into the
topping, etc.

TOPPING

¼ c. brown sugar
¼ c. whole wheat flour
¼ c. raw wheat germ
¼ c. oatmeal
1 T. soy flour
1 t. nutritional yeast
1 t. cinnamon
¼ c. margarine or butter

Mix together dry ingredients. Cut in margarine until mixture resembles crumbs.

GREEN TOMATO MINCEMEAT

Yield: Approx. 1 gallon

8 c. chopped green tomatoes
8 c. chopped tart apples
6 c. raisins, chopped
5 c. sugar (or much less, to taste)
2 heaping t. cinnamon
1 t. ground cloves
1 t. allspice
2 t. grated orange peel
1 lemon (grated peel and juice)
½ c. cider vinegar
Salt to taste

Combine all ingredients in a large, heavy
saucepan. Simmer 2 hours, stirring frequently, or until mixture is of desired consistency. Correct seasonings. Freeze or can.
Can be used as an ice-cream topping, in
pies, or in mincemeat bread.

GINGERSNAPS

Yield: 3 dozen cookies

1½ c. whole wheat pastry flour
¼ c. brown sugar, firmly packed
1 t. baking powder
1½ t. ginger
¼ c. wheat germ
¼ t. salt
¼ c. butter or margarine
1 egg
3 T. old-fashioned molasses

Mix dry ingredients together. With a pastry
blender, cut in butter until mixture resembles crumbs. Add the egg and molasses and
stir well with a fork. Let chill one half hour.
Preheat oven to 375°. Flour a pastry cloth
well and with a covered, well-floured rolling
pin, roll the dough out about ⅛ inch thick.
Cut with small round cookie cutter, and
place on a greased baking sheet. Bake for 5 to
10 minutes or until done. Remove immediately to a wire rack for cooling.

GREEN TOMATO MINCE PIE

Yield: 1 pie

3 to 4 c. Green Tomato Mincemeat
1 recipe double pie crust

Preheat oven to 425°. Line 9-inch pie plate
with crust. Spoon mincemeat into crust. Roll
out dough for top, making design in center
through which steam can escape. Place top
crust on prepared pie, firmly pressing dough
together around edges. Trim and flute edges
as desired. Bake for 8 minutes. Lower heat to
325° and continue baking for 20 minutes or
until crust is lightly browned.

YOGURT ORANGE SHERBET

Yield: About 1 pint

1 6-oz. can frozen orange juice
concentrate
1 to 2 c. plain yogurt (to taste)

Pour juice concentrate into mixing bowl. Stir
in yogurt until you like the taste. Pour into
ice cube tray or other freezer bowl. Serve
when firm. If you won't be using it right
away, cover the sherbet as soon as it is
frozen.

*Photograph opposite:
Rhubarb (or Apple) Crumble*

RHUBARB CAKE

Yield: 12 to 16 pieces

5 T. butter or margarine
¾ c. brown sugar, firmly packed
1 egg
½ c. yogurt or buttermilk
¼ t. salt
1 c. whole wheat flour
2½ t. baking powder
¼ c. non-instant powdered milk
¼ c. raw wheat germ
1½ c. chopped rhubarb (or apple)

Preheat oven to 350°. Cream butter and sugar together; beat in egg until fluffy. Add yogurt. Mix dry ingredients together and stir into egg mixture, beating until thoroughly blended. Stir in rhubarb. Pour into lightly greased 8 x 8-inch cake pan. Sprinkle Topping evenly over batter. Bake for 30 to 40 minutes or until top springs back when pressed lightly.

TOPPING

¼ c. brown sugar
¼ t. cinnamon
¼ c. raw wheat germ
⅓ c. chopped nuts

Mix ingredients with a fork.

DATE NUT BARS

Yield: 12 to 16 bars

¾ c. brown sugar, firmly packed
¼ c. margarine or butter
2 eggs
¾ c. whole wheat flour
¼ c. raw wheat germ
½ t. baking powder
½ t. salt
1 c. pitted and chopped dates
½ c. chopped nuts
½ t. vanilla

Preheat oven to 350°. Cream sugar and margarine. Beat in eggs until light and fluffy. Stir dry ingredients together; add gradually to egg mixture, beating well. Stir in dates, nuts, and vanilla. Pour into well-greased 9 x 9-inch cake pan. Bake 30 minutes, or until top springs back when touched lightly. Cut into squares while hot.

MOLASSES-WHEAT GERM COOKIES

Yield: 3 to 4 dozen cookies

¾ c. margarine
¾ c. brown sugar, firmly packed
¼ c. old-fashioned molasses
1 egg
½ c. non-instant powdered milk
1½ c. whole wheat pastry flour
¾ c. raw wheat germ
2 t. baking powder
½ t. cloves
1 t. cinnamon

Cream margarine and sugar together; add molasses. Beat in egg. Mix dry ingredients together and add to batter. Stir well. Chill about one hour. Preheat oven to 350°. Roll dough into 1-inch balls and place on lightly greased baking sheet. Press flat with the smooth bottom of a glass dipped in flour. If desired, raisins may be used to decorate the cookies.

Bake for 10 to 12 minutes or until lightly browned. Remove after a few moments from baking sheet to wire rack to finish cooling.

PUMPKIN AND RAISIN COOKIES

Yield: 5 dozen cookies

1 c. cooked pumpkin or winter squash, mashed
⅔ c. brown sugar
½ c. vegetable oil
1 large egg
2 c. whole wheat flour
2 t. baking powder
1 t. cinnamon
¼ t. cloves
¼ t. nutmeg
½ t. salt
1 t. baking soda dissolved in 1 t. milk
1 c. raisins
½ c. chopped nuts or raw sunflower seeds
1 t. vanilla

Preheat oven to 350°. Thoroughly combine pumpkin, sugar, oil, and egg. (Use blender if pumpkin is lumpy.) Stir together flour, baking powder, spices, and salt. Add to pumpkin mixture along with dissolved soda and mix well. Stir in raisins, nuts, and vanilla. Drop by teaspoonfuls on lightly greased cookie sheets. Bake 10 to 12 minutes or until done. Cool on wire rack.

INDIAN PUDDING

Yield: 4 servings

1½ c. milk
2 T. cornmeal
1 egg, beaten
¼ c. old-fashioned molasses
2 T. brown sugar
½ t. cinnamon
¼ t. salt
¼ t. ginger
¼ t. nutmeg
½ c. wheat germ

Preheat oven to 325°. In a medium-sized heavy pan over medium heat, scald milk (150°). Gradually stir in cornmeal. Cook for approximately 8 minutes, stirring frequently, until mixture is well cooked and thickened. Remove from heat. Combine the rest of the ingredients. Stir the milk mixture into the other ingredients, mixing well. Pour into lightly greased 1½-quart baking dish. Place in a large pan half filled with hot water. Bake for about 1 hour or until table knife inserted in center comes out nearly clean. Serve hot or cold, plain or with yogurt.

EASY CHEESY APPLE PIE

Yield: 6 to 8 servings

5 to 6 apples, sliced and cored (don't peel)
2 T. apple juice or water
2 T. honey (if using sweet apples, omit honey)
¼ c. raisins
¼ c. currants (or more raisins)
2 c. rolled oats
¼ c. unsalted peanuts
½ c. chopped walnuts
¼ c. sunflower seeds (optional)
½ t. salt
¼ lb. grated Cheddar cheese

In a heavy, tightly covered pan over low heat, cook apples, juice, and honey for about 15 minutes or until apples are just beginning to get soft. Preheat oven to 350°. Pour apple mixture into a 9-inch pie plate. Pour currants and raisins on top. Mix together the rest of the ingredients except cheese and pour on top of pie. Bake for 10 minutes or until topping is browned. Pour grated cheese on top of pie and bake for an additional 5 to 10 minutes or until all cheese has melted. Best served hot.

STEAMED CARROT PUDDING

Yield: 8 to 10 servings

1 c. whole wheat flour
1 t. baking soda
¾ c. brown sugar, firmly packed
1 t. allspice
1 t. cinnamon
1 t. nutmeg
1 c. seedless raisins
1 c. coarsely chopped walnuts or other nuts
1 c. grated carrot
1 c. grated potatoes
2 eggs, beaten
2 T. margarine or butter, melted and cooled

Stir together dry ingredients. Add raisins and nuts. Stir carrots, potatoes, eggs, and butter together and add dry ingredients. Spoon into a well-greased 1½ quart mold. Cover mold tightly with waxed paper held on by a rubber band. Place into steamer or pan with a rack. Fill pan with hot water so that mold is only half submerged. Steam, covered, on top of stove over medium heat for 1½ hours or until done. Batter will rise and be firm to the touch when done. Remove from pan when cool.

BROWN RICE CUSTARD PUDDING

Yield: 6 to 8 servings

4 eggs
1 t. vanilla
1 t. nutmeg
1 qt. whole milk
½ c. non-instant powdered milk
2 T. honey
¼ c. raw wheat germ
½-1 c. cooked brown rice
½ c. raisins
⅛ t. salt

Preheat oven to 325°. Beat eggs well, stir in vanilla and nutmeg. In a large, separate bowl, beat milks together until smooth. Add honey. Stir in the rest of the ingredients, mixing well. Stir in the eggs gently but thoroughly. Pour into a well-greased, 2-quart baking dish; sprinkle nutmeg on top. Put baking dish in a large baking pan nearly filled with hot water and bake for about 45 minutes or until knife inserted in the center comes out clean.

THE MEINERS' TOFU "CHEESE" CAKE

Yield: 8 to 10 servings

GRAHAM CRACKER CRUST

1 c. finely crushed graham cracker crumbs
3 T. melted margarine

Combine crumbs and margarine; reserve 1 tablespoon for topping. Press remaining crumbs in the bottom of a 9-inch round cake pan. Bake in a 350° oven for 6 minutes; cool.

FILLING

1 lb. 4-oz. medium firm tofu (soybean curd)
2 eggs
½ c. brown sugar, packed
2 T. lemon juice
1 1-inch piece lemon peel
1 t. vanilla
2 ripe bananas
1 20-oz. can crushed pineapple, drained

Preheat oven to 325°. Drain tofu, pat dry with paper towels. Place eggs, sugar, juice, peel, and vanilla in blender. Break tofu and bananas into chunks and add half to blender. Cover and blend until smooth. Add remaining banana and tofu chunks to blender; cover and blend again until smooth. Stir in drained pineapple (don't blend) and pour into cooled crust. Sprinkle reserved crumbs on top. Bake for 1 hour or just until center jiggles slightly when pan is gently shaken. Cool on a wire rack and chill until serving time.

CARROT CAKE

Yield: One 9″ x 9″ cake

1¼ c. whole wheat pastry flour
2 t. baking powder
1 T. nutritional yeast
½ t. cinnamon
⅛ t. salt
¾ c. vegetable oil
1 c. brown sugar, firmly packed
2 eggs
1 c. finely grated carrots

Preheat oven to 350°. Thoroughly mix together flour, baking powder, yeast, cinnamon and salt. In a large mixing bowl, combine the sugar and oil, mixing well. Add eggs one at a time, beating well after each

Photograph opposite:
Carrot Cake

addition. Add dry ingredients gradually. Finally, add grated carrots, blending well. Pour into a well-greased 9 x 9-inch cake pan or loaf tin. Bake for 35 to 45 minutes or until top springs back when pressed lightly and edges pull away from the side of the pan. If icing is desired, use the following:

NUT ICING

2 T. softened butter or margarine
3 oz. cream cheese (room temperature)
2 to 3 T. honey (to taste)
½ t. vanilla
¼ c. raw wheat germ
¼ c. non-instant powdered milk
¾ c. chopped walnuts

Blend butter and cream cheese until smooth. Add honey and vanilla. Stir in wheat germ and powdered milk. If frosting is too thick, add a little more honey. Spread onto cooled cake and pour walnuts over evenly.

KATHY'S APPLE-DATE PIE

Yield: 8 servings

2 eggs
½ c. brown sugar
2 t. whole wheat flour
¼ t. salt
1 t. grated lemon rind
1 t. lemon juice
1 c. sour cream
⅓ c. finely chopped dates (or raisins or currants)
3 c. sliced, tart apples
1 9-inch, unbaked, deep-dish pastry crust

Preheat oven to 400°. Beat the eggs until frothy and stir in sugar, flour, salt, lemon rind, and lemon juice. Fold in sour cream. Finally fold in dates and apples. Mix well and pour into pastry crust. Bake for 10 minutes. Sprinkle Topping onto pie and continue baking 30 to 35 minutes or until topping is lightly browned and filling is set. Chill until served.

TOPPING

⅓ c. brown sugar
½ c. whole wheat flour
½ t. grated nutmeg
1 T. butter

Combine dry ingredients. Cut in butter until mixture is crumbly.

PEPPERNUTS

Yield: 7 dozen cookies

1 c. old-fashioned molasses
1 c. brown sugar
1 c. non-hydrogenated lard or shortening
2 t. cloves
1 T. cinnamon
1 T. anise seed (crushed with a rolling pin)
1 c. chopped nuts
2 t. baking soda, dissolved in 1 t. water
½ c. soy flour
1 T. nutritional yeast
2 c. whole wheat flour
1½ c. unbleached flour

Preheat oven to 300°. Thoroughly cream molasses, sugar, and lard. Mix in spices, then the rest of the ingredients until thoroughly blended. If dough is not stiff enough, add more flour. With floured hands, roll into balls approximately 1-inch diameter. Bake for 10 minutes or until lightly browned. Cool thoroughly on wire rack.

YOGURT APPLE PIE

Yield: 6 to 8 servings

3-4 apples (enough to fill an 8″ pie plate) Soft apples such as McIntosh or Jonathan work well
1 T. whole wheat pastry flour
2 T. non-instant powdered milk
1 T. raw wheat germ
¼ c. brown sugar
½ c. yogurt or sour cream
1 egg, beaten

Preheat oven to 350°. Wash and cut apples into eighths, removing core. Mix milk, flour, wheat germ, and sugar together. Add yogurt and stir well. Mix in egg, then apples. Pour into an 8-inch pie plate. Pour Topping evenly over top of pie, dot with butter. Bake for 45 minutes or until custard is set.

TOPPING

¼ c. brown sugar
1 T. whole wheat pastry flour
2 T. raw wheat germ
½ t. cinnamon

With a fork, mix together all ingredients.

RAISIN YEAST CAKE

Yield: 1 large or 2 small loaf cakes

2¼ t. or 1 pkg. active dry yeast
1⅓ c. lukewarm water
1 t. honey
2½ c. whole wheat pastry flour
¼ t. salt
¼ c. honey
½ t. cinnamon
½ t. ginger
½ t. nutmeg
1 c. raisins (or a mixture of currants and raisins)
1 t. grated orange rind
½ c. melted butter or margarine
2 eggs, slightly beaten

Mix yeast, water, and 1 teaspoon honey together and let stand for 15 minutes. Mix flour and salt together; stir into the yeast mixture. Cover the bowl with a towel, leave in a warm place (80°) for 1½ hours to rise. Stir into the dough the additional honey, spices, and fruit. Add the rind and butter and beat well. Finally, beat in the eggs. Divide in half, if desired. Place batter into two, small, well-greased bread tins or a 1-pound coffee can or larger tin. Cover and let rise for 30 minutes or until doubled. Preheat oven to 350°. Brush the top with milk and bake for 45 minutes or until done. Larger loaf will take longer. Remove from tins to cool.

DOUBLE PIE CRUST

Yield: Two 9 or 10-inch crusts

1½ c. whole wheat pastry flour
¼ c. raw wheat germ
½ t. salt
¾ c. margarine
2 T. (approximately) water

Have all ingredients cold. Mix together flour, wheat germ, and salt in a large mixing bowl. Cut in margarine with a pastry blender until mixture resembles fine crumbs. Add the water and stir gently with a fork until dough forms. Divide dough in half and roll out on a well-floured pastry cloth. Bake according to recipe specifications. If you want an unfilled, baked pie crust, prick crust with fork several times and bake in a 425° oven for about 10 minutes or until crust is done.

Note: Unbaked pastry shells freeze well. Just thaw before baking.

CAROB BROWNIES

Yield: Approximately 3½ dozen

- 1 c. margarine
- 2 c. honey
- 1 c. carob powder
- ½ t. salt
- 4 eggs
- 2 t. baking powder
- 2 T. soy flour, sifted
- 2 T. raw wheat germ
- 2 c. whole wheat pastry flour
- 1 t. vanilla
- 1 c. chopped nuts

Preheat oven to 350°. In a small pan over medium heat, melt margarine. Remove from heat and stir in honey, carob powder, and salt. In a large mixing bowl, beat eggs well. Stir in baking powder, soy flour, and wheat germ. Add carob mixture and beat well. Stir in flour and vanilla. Stir in nuts. Pour mixture into a well-greased 10 x 14-inch cake pan. Bake about 40 minutes or until toothpick inserted in center comes out clean.

BANANA-MIXED GRAIN COOKIES

Yield: 4 to 5 dozen cookies

- ¾ c. margarine
- ¾ c. brown sugar
- 1 egg
- 1 c. mashed ripe banana
- 1 t. lemon or vanilla extract
- 1 t. salt
- 1 t. baking powder
- ½ t. nutmeg
- ¾ t. cinnamon
- 1¼ c. whole wheat flour
- ¼ c. raw wheat germ
- 1½ c. raw mixed-grain cereal or oatmeal
- ½ c. chopped walnuts or other nuts or raisins

Beat margarine, sugar, and egg until light and fluffy. Stir in banana and flavoring until smooth. Add salt, baking powder, and spices and stir thoroughly. Slowly mix in dry ingredients until well combined, adding nuts last. Chill for at least 1 hour. Preheat oven to 375° Drop batter by teaspoonfuls onto lightly greased baking sheets. Bake 10 to 12 minutes or until done. Cool on wire rack.

CHRIS'S OATMEAL-RAISIN COOKIES

Yield: Approximately 6 dozen

- 1 c. margarine or shortening
- 1 c. brown sugar, firmly packed
- ¾ c. honey
- 3 eggs
- 2¾ c. whole wheat pastry flour
- ½ c. raw wheat germ
- 1 t. baking soda
- 1 t. baking powder
- 1 t. cloves
- 2 t. cinnamon
- 1 t. allspice
- 1 t. apple pie spice
- 1 t. nutmeg
- 1 t. vanilla
- 1 c. thick, unsweetened applesauce
- 8 c. oatmeal
- 4 c. raisins (or more, as desired)

Preheat oven to 350°. Cream together margarine and sugar; add honey and eggs, and blend thoroughly. In a separate bowl, mix together all the dry ingredients except oatmeal and raisins. Stir into the egg mixture. When thoroughly mixed, add vanilla, applesauce, oatmeal, and raisins. (Portions of the dough can be frozen at this point; thaw when ready to bake and proceed with recipe.) Drop dough from a teaspoon onto ungreased baking sheets. Bake 8 to 10 minutes or until done; remove immediately from tins and allow to cool on wire racks.

Glossary

Agar-agar: an edible seaweed gelatin; available in flakes, bars, and granules.

Braise: to cook by browning in vegetable oil and then simmering, covered, with a small amount of added liquid.

Bran: outer coating of the wheat kernel; high in B vitamins.

Buckwheat: also called kasha; not a wheat but from a hardy herb.

Bulgur or bulghur: cracked wheat.

Carob: a chocolate substitute made from the St. John's plant. It does not produce the allergic reactions that chocolate does, is low in fat, and contains no caffeine. It does not taste like chocolate.

Graham flour: another name for whole grain or whole wheat flour. The best graham flour is stone ground because this process does not generate the heat that kills many of the nutrients.

Mince: to cut up into very fine pieces.

Non-hydrogenated: preferable to hydrogenated foods and includes oils which are processed with hydrogen to produce a solid fat.

Non-instant powdered milk: has more nutrients than instant; is usually more satisfactory in baking.

Nutritional yeast: another name for brewer's yeast and can be consumed raw, unlike baking or active yeast. Can be added to foods to add protein and the vitamin B complex.

Old-fashioned molasses: unsulphured, dark molasses.

Organically grown: foods which are grown without chemical fertilizers or pesticides.

Purée: mashed into a pulp after cooking, usually in a blender or sieve.

Sauté: to cook quickly in a small amount of oil, turning frequently.

Simmer: to cook just at or below boiling point; bubbles rise gently to the surface.

Tamari: a soy sauce concentrate available in natural food stores. Commercial soy sauce is not really a substitute.

Tempura: deep-fried, battered foods.

Tofu: soybean curd. Made from soy products, it is very bland and blends well with seasonings. Some people call it soy cheese.

Unbleached flour: creamy white flour which has not been bleached with chemicals.

Wheat germ: the part of the grain from which the new plant can grow. Raw wheat germ should be used when possible, because some of the nutrients in toasted wheat germ have already been harmed by heat. Wheat germ contains a high quality protein and B vitamins.

Whole wheat flour: flour ground from the whole grain, containing the endosperm, bran, and germ; it is milled from hard wheat.

Whole wheat pastry flour: more finely ground than plain whole wheat flour; it is milled from soft wheat. Unfortunately, it differs from mill to mill.

SUBSTITUTIONS	
1 cup buttermilk or sour cream	= 1 cup yogurt
¼ cup cocoa	= ¼ cup carob powder
1 cup granulated sugar	= 1 cup honey in yeast breads; ⅞ cup honey in cookies and cakes; reduce liquid in recipe by 3 tablespoons.
	or 1 cup firmly packed light brown sugar
	or 1 cup maple syrup; reduce liquid in recipe by ¼ cup
1 cup all-purpose flour	= ⅝ cup oat flour plus ⅜ cup rice flour
	or ⅞ cup whole wheat flour
	or 1 cup unbleached flour
	or 2/3 cup whole wheat flour plus 1/3 cup wheat germ
	or ¾ cup whole wheat flour plus ¼ cup bran
	or ⅞ cup whole wheat flour plus 2 tablespoons soy flour (reduce baking temperature about 25° when adding soy flour)
2 cups water plus 1 T. unflavored gelatin	= 2 cups water plus 2 to 3 tablespoons agar-agar
1 T. fresh herbs	= 1 teaspoons dried herbs
1 cup white, enriched, or converted rice	= 1 cup brown rice

Photograph opposite:
Chris's Oatmeal Raisin Cookies, p. 61

Index